"I Belong to the Working Class"

"I BELONG

The Unfinished

TO THE

Autobiography of

WORKING

Rose Pastor Stokes

CLASS"

Edited by Herbert Shapiro and David L. Sterling

THE UNIVERSITY OF GEORGIA PRESS   ATHENS AND LONDON

921 STOKES

I belong to the working class; the unfinished autobiography of Rose Stok

© 1992 by the University of Georgia Press
Athens, Georgia 30602

All rights reserved
Designed by Erin Kirk
Set in Goudy Old Style by Tseng Information Systems, Inc.
Printed and bound by Braun-Brumfield
The paper in this book meets the guidelines for
permanence and durability of the Committee on
Production Guidelines for Book Longevity of the
Council on Library Resources.

Printed in the United States of America

96   95   94   93   92   C   5   4   3   2   1

Library of Congress Cataloging in Publication Data

Stokes, Rose Pastor, 1879–1933.
I belong to the working class : the unfinished autobiography of
Rose Pastor Stokes / edited by Herbert Shapiro and David L. Sterling.
p.   cm.
Includes bibliographical references and index.
ISBN 0-8203-1383-1 (alk. paper)
1. Stokes, Rose Pastor, 1879–1933.   2. Feminists—United States—
Biography.   3. Women socialists—United States—Biography.
I. Shapiro, Herbert.   II. Sterling, David L.   III. Title.
HQ1413.S69A3   1992
305.42′092—dc20
[B]   91-14089
                                                           CIP

British Library Cataloging in Publication Data available

Contents

Acknowledgments

The editors of this volume wish to acknowledge the assistance provided by several research libraries in the course of preparing the manuscript for publication. We are particularly indebted to Yale University Library for the permission granted to publish this work. Most helpful also was the Tamiment Library, New York University and the interlibrary loan department of the University of Cincinnati's Langsam Library.

We owe thanks to Judith Schiff, chief research archivist at Yale University Library's manuscripts and archives department for having originally called the existence of the autobiography to our attention and for her consistent encouragement of the project. We were helped, too, by information provided by Nancy Lyon, RLIN/ORBIS coordinator at the Sterling Library. The assistance provided by Sally Moffitt, associate librarian at the Langsam Library, was extremely helpful. We are grateful, as well, for the aid furnished by the staff members of the Klau Library and the American Jewish Archives at the Hebrew Union College. Arthur and Pearl Zipser, authors of the recently published biography *Fire and Grace*, generously responded to several questions about the life of Rose Pastor Stokes. Thanks are owed also to John M. Whitcomb of Dedham, Massachusetts, who graciously shared his recollections of Rose Pastor Stokes.

The skilled work of Heather Hall in preparing the word-processed text of the manuscript is much appreciated. The editing of this book was facilitated by a grant-in-aid awarded by the University Research Council of the University of Cincinnati and that assistance is gratefully acknowledged.

The editors express appreciation for the loving encouragement provided by their family members, Judith, Mark, and Nina Shapiro and Jennifer and Vanessa Sterling.

In preparing the autobiography the editors have retained the style of the text as originally written by Rose Pastor Stokes, including the frequent use of ellipses to denote an incompleteness of thought or to set off a reminiscence. In a few instances of inconsistent punctuation that might be misleading to the reader the usage has been made uniform, and where the significance of persons cited in the text is unclear appropriate information has been provided in footnotes.

Introduction

Rose Harriet Wieslander, or as she later became known to us, Rose
Pastor Stokes, was born in the town of Augustova, Poland, on July 18,
1879. Her death, caused by cancer, came on June 20, 1933, in Frankfurt am Main, Germany. Those with any awareness of labor history or
the record of the emancipatory struggles of American women know of
such figures as Harriet Tubman, Emma Goldman, Margaret Sanger, Jane
Addams, and Elizabeth Gurley Flynn, but Rose Pastor Stokes's image
has faded from our recollection and only in 1990 has a first biography
appeared.[1] Her life, however, offers us a window on the experience of
someone who vividly expressed many of the critical trends of her time,
who underwent remarkable changes in direction while unswervingly
holding to her basic commitments. At one point in her life Stokes said
that other than her marriage "there is nothing remarkable for me to
tell of my life. I was but one of an overwhelming number of working
women when I came to this country and went into a cigar factory."[2]
Indeed her life's story is that of a woman of the working class. But it is
also the life of someone who passionately committed herself to making
a better, more humane world, who lifted herself out of the struggle for
daily economic survival, marrying James Graham Phelps Stokes of one
of America's great millionaire, patrician families, but never forgetting

her origins. She could not bring herself to be merely another American "success" story.

Rose Pastor Stokes's life was marked by contradiction and bold breaks with the past. In her youth her daily routine was shaped by the misery of sweatshop conditions and the grinding poverty of her family, but her imagination was gripped by the accounts of royalty she read in the Lambs's *Tales From Shakespeare.* Her allegiance was to the workers, but she was determined to lead a life other than that of the shop worker. After leaving Cleveland she immersed herself in the culture and politics of New York's immigrant East Side, but marriage would take her into the world of the Protestant gentry, a world in which she never would comfortably fit. For years she deferred to her husband's intellectual attainments but came to be disturbed that for him mingling with the workers was a tiring duty, whereas for her it was emotional sustenance. As a socialist she spoke often before middle-class intellectuals and professionals, where the contest was one of ideas, but she was most drawn to the workers' economic struggles, to the open confrontation of the strike. Described by historian June Sochen as a "feminist," Stokes wrote shortly before her death, "I have never been a feminist as such," but for a time she was a fervent activist in the birth control movement, and in her early journalistic writings she sought to enhance the dignity of the women workers for whom she wrote.[3] Her first response to American entrance into World War I was to join with the ex-socialists who endorsed the Wilson policies, but in the fall of 1917 she endorsed an antiwar candidate in the New York mayoralty election and wholeheartedly embraced the Bolshevik revolution. Within a period of months she was invited to dine with President Wilson and indicted for alleged violation of the Espionage Act. Her husband viewed American supporters of communism as "ingrates," but Rose Pastor Stokes participated in the 1919 founding convention of the Communist party. For a time in her life she moved among the rich, but she became a revolutionary who died in poverty. Beneath the level of appearances, what gave consistency to Rose Pastor Stokes's life was that she would not be pressured to conform to someone else's mold; she would express her own view of the world and was prepared to pay the cost of speaking truth to power. In her commitment to challenging convention, in her insistence on self-definition, she was one of the pioneers in asserting the public role of American women. Her resolute effort to reconcile individual freedom with loyalty to the working class places her among the representative figures in American labor and radical history.

The early years of Rose Pastor Stokes are a classic story of the immigrant and a vivid reminder of the cruelties of industrial conditions at the turn of the century. At the age of three, leaving behind the *shtetl* life of Augustova in the wake of pogroms further menacing the always insecure position of Jews under Czarist rule, Rose was taken by her mother to the East End slum district of London. The family experienced flashes of hope that things would improve, that opportunity would rescue them from the hunger and wretched housing they encountered. But they were not to be separated from the lot of their fellows. Rose recalled listening to the talk about shop conditions, the inhumanity of the "masters." Her mother became another of the shop workers, laboring twelve hours a day, taking a bit of satisfaction from being able to look through the windows to the world outside. The master, however, unable to tolerate this distraction, whitewashed the windows, and in response the workers went on strike, Rose's mother in the lead. Rose remembered the victory the workers won. Her child's eye was absorbing the realities of working-class life, and soon she too would join the work force. Whatever Rose Pastor Stokes became in her life she could never have forgotten that she was one of the child laborers, exploited as were her elders. With her mother she worked at home, making satin bows for ladies' slippers. She recalled attending a May Day demonstration at Hyde Park, vaguely comprehending what was happening.

In 1890, Rose, her mother, and stepbrother Maurice, made the voyage to America, joining stepfather Israel Pastor in Cleveland. In their new home the Pastors were trapped in poverty, with Israel barely earning enough for survival in his trade of junk peddler, and Rose, at the age of eleven, compelled to go to work in a cigar factory. This was in an era, now almost entirely vanished in the United States, when cigar making was the work of hand labor. After a time she was to be employed in a "buckeye" shop, a factory operating in the owner's home. In other words, as Rose later wrote, she was now at work in a sweatshop. Like millions of others, the Pastors felt the severe impact of the 1893 depression. The family's hopes for a better life in America were mocked by the economic storm that depressed wages below subsistence and brought ruin to Israel's peddling venture. Sinking into despair and alcoholism, after a cycle of departures and returns, Israel Pastor permanently abandoned his family. For Rose the discipline of routinized manual labor substituted for formal education, but she came to know the struggle for existence and survival that was at the core of American capitalism. She also had the experience of witnessing the class division existing within ethnic communities. She worked in the "buckeyes" with other Jews, but her employers were Jews as well and this common ethnicity was no shield against exploitation.

While working in the Cleveland cigar shops Rose became involved in an unsuccessful effort to unionize the unskilled workers. The workers rented a hall and held meetings, but their request to enroll as members in the AFL-affiliated Cigar Makers' International Union was rejected. They had run up against the policy of AFL president Samuel Gompers of emphasizing the organization of a more privileged stratum of skilled workers.[4]

In 1901 Rose found an outlet for her creative energies that shortly would enable her to leave the drudgery of the cigar factory. Encountering a copy of the New York Yiddish newspaper, the *Jewish Daily News* (*Yiddishes Tageblatt*), she was drawn by the invitation to write letters for publication. Her first letter appeared in the July 22, 1901, issue of the paper. She wrote a whimsical account of what impelled her to write, yet mentioned she rolled two hundred fewer cigars in order to finish the letter. She signed her full name "Rose Harriet Pastor" and gave her home address.[5] She was urged to write more letters and she did so; her columns became regular features of the English-language page of the newspaper. In March 1903 she left the shop and moved to New York, joining the *Jewish Daily News*'s staff.

Shortly after coming to the city Rose wrote of the first impressions that New York made upon her. She noticed the "dinky" horse cars that very slowly made their way through the city, but found that in New York only the cars and the telephones operated slowly. The fastest of everything were the people, "they are forever in a hurry and those who have nothing else to be busy about are busy just because they are in New York city." Her attention was caught by the ghetto market on Hester Street, and she reported that all down the street, "as far as the eye could see, on either side, crowding the sidewalks were women, women and women." There was the hubbub coming from the pushcart peddlers hawking their wares. All this Rose Pastor found to be a novel sight. She had earlier seen Petticoat Lane in London, but she observed she had been too young for that famous market to have made any lasting impression upon her. She provided a colorful account of the selling that went on in the fish market, the vigorous bargaining between customers and peddlers. But there was also pathos in her account, the sad story of the elderly woman forced to sell candles to eke out a living because one of her two daughters was too poor to help her and the other, married to a rich man, would give her nothing. Rose also observed the many itinerant workmen who stood about hoping for some odd jobs. "I walked away rapidly," she wrote, "looking at those men opened up the misery of their home life to me—their wives, their children. I felt the deep world-sorrow."[6]

Rose's articles in the *Jewish Daily News* discussed a variety of topics, but most of the pieces revolved around themes of dignity, self-respect, and moral obligation. In an article appearing in the October 9, 1901, issue she wrote: "I want you to be working *girls* not working *machines*. I want you all to be working, thinking women, not mere automatons!" There was no reason for the shop women for whom she wrote not to read the best books and think the best thoughts. She went on to say: "One of your own factory-girls appeals to you *in the name of the factory-girl* to rise! to rise to a beautiful, noble womanhood!"[7] Reflected in her pieces was also a sense of anguish over the human condition, and she touched upon what her readers had so often experienced for themselves. "It is a sad world, this," she wrote, "so much pain and sorrow; so much poverty and suffering is the lot of those who are perhaps, God's best beloved. And, oh, how it clutches me at the heart-strings—the thought that all this pain and misery is man's through his brother-man."[8]

Rose Pastor offered her readers moral instruction, a commitment to values that could be relied upon in a chaotic world. She offered advice on how to distinguish true from false friendship. The friendship that was true and genuine abides. A vital part of the moral life was showing affection and love to one's mother. The daughter was urged to honor and confide in mother. One's mother would not always be there. "The world is unsympathetic," she wrote, and it must be remembered "there are times when sympathy is as necessary as the air we breathe." She advocated integrity and giving of one's self to others. The person, she wrote, who prays best, prays for usefulness and helpfulness, prays for help in upholding truth "under any and all circumstances." God will help us, she declared, if her readers sought to be "good, dutiful, loving daughters; good, earnest, noble, genuine women." Kindness was a virtue to be cultivated. "Fill the cup of happiness for others," she wrote, "and there will be enough overflowing to fill yours to the brim." Hatred was wrong, even hatred of the employer, and she noted that if one hated one's work, one would hate the employer, foolishly holding him accountable "for all the misery of the masses."[9]

Regarding social relationships Rose's readers were advised not to be loud and hail-fellow but rather to be natural. Young women should not meet young men on street corners, but should rather bring them home. These columns manifested a respect for traditional values. This respect extended to an acceptance of American nationalism. On the occasion of one Decoration Day, Rose editorialized about "this glorious country, where you were welcomed with open arms to liberty and life, to love and tolerance, to light and hope." [10]

The 1903 Russian massacre of Jews at Kishineff evoked a fiery response from Rose Pastor in which were combined notes of Jewish nationalism with indignation at American counterparts of the pogrom spirit. Writing under the heading "Next Year in Jerusalem" she declared that the massacre "will be the bugle-call that will summon all American Jewry to enter the Zionist ranks to which it will respond with quickening pulse and leaping heart. Zionism is no longer a wild dream—an idle fancy; Zionism is a vital and powerful factor which is making itself felt, everywhere." But she also wrote in an editorial, "Kishineffing It," that Jews in the United States were also obliged to protest anti-Semitism and anti-black violence. "Jew-baiting and Negro-lynching," she stated, "are two blunders well worth being freed from; Kishineffing outside of the land of Kishineff is a greater blot upon civilization than in that 'hell's kitchen,' Russia." [11]

In December 1903, responding to a reader's plea for advice about her socialist lover's importunings for a "free love" relationship, Rose expressed her rejection of "free love" while avoiding a stereotyped view of the radicals. She flatly urged "Dinah" to leave her lover and refuse to see him again. She referred to the "demoralized socialist circles" that existed on the lower East Side, but also added: "There is no Socialist, who is also an honest man, who would not marry the woman he truly loves. And there is no man, socialist, any other 'ist' or no 'ist,' at all, who preaches the doctrine of 'free love' to a woman, who has not, at the same time, the thought in his mind to desert her after she yields to his wishes, after she foolishly throws away the 'immediate jewel of her soul.' " Rose outlined two images of the socialists. On the one hand "are some socialists who, though they are discontented and bitter, still are moral and would not poison any good woman's life for the mere gratification of a passion." There were socialists whose belief was "of a hopeful kind, whose hearts are filled with love and tenderness for all humanity;

they are the socialists who, should the millenium come, would be the most fit to receive it." But she also found another variety of socialists, those "who are met with in certain cafes on the East Side and who may be heard at all times airing their grievances, condemning all present institutions, and expressing a longing for the love of a woman who will cling to them no matter what betide (without that woman expecting such a bauble as a marriage ring, of course!), those socialists are all that are moral pests. The further distance a young woman put between herself and them, the better for her." [12]

In the course of her work for the *Jewish Daily News* Rose was sent to interview various East Side personalities, including many of the sponsors and operators of the various settlement houses, philanthropic institutions devoted to the betterment of the immigrant population. One of those she was assigned to interview was James Graham Phelps Stokes of the University Settlement. A member of a distinguished and wealthy American family, a graduate of Yale's Sheffield Scientific School and of the medical college at Columbia, Stokes had set upon a course of devoting himself to improving the conditions of the poor. Faced with his father's opposition to his initial plan of becoming a medical missionary in Africa, Stokes, as Allen Davis observes, "became instead a missionary to the Lower East Side." [13] Rose Pastor was much impressed with the man she was sent to interview. Questioned about a reported division within the University Settlement, Stokes denied he planned to establish a rival to the University Settlement, but stressed his belief that those who directly participated in the work of the organization should have more say as to how it was run. They should have as much involvement in the decision-making process as the "uptown friends who have little personal knowledge of the needs or opportunities involved."

In her interview, Rose briefly outlined some of Stokes's essential beliefs. "Mr. Stokes," she asserted, "believes in the furtherance of movements to better the condition of the working classes. He does not believe that the Settlement should be a sort of general almoner. He believes that Settlements should be run on broad lines; and that they should do their utmost to arouse public interest in social and industrial conditions, public recognition of existing evils, and public support for movements destined to secure improved conditions and to promote the public welfare." Rose quoted Stokes as saying his religion had led him "to recognize the duty of social service" and that he shared the desire of social workers to improve social conditions. He had no desire to make converts to a particular religious creed. Stokes recognized that misunderstanding and misinterpretation of motives were inevitable, but Rose reported that Stokes manifested "an unutterable longing to change the world in this one respect, so that none might suffer." As she saw Graham Stokes in that interview he was clearly a hero figure. She summarized her impressions thus: "Mr. Stokes is a deep, strong thinker. His youthful face 'takes' by virtue of its frank, earnest and kind expression. . . . Mr. Stokes loves humanity for its own sake and as he speaks on with the sincerity which is the keynote of his character, you feel how the whole heart and soul of the man is filled with 'welt schmerz'; you feel that, metaphorically speaking, he has sown his black young curls with bleaching cares of half a million men, already. Mr. Stokes is very tall, and, I believe, six foot of the most thorough democracy. A thoroughbred gentleman, a scholar and a son of a millionaire, he is a man of the common people, even as Lincoln was. He is a plain man and makes one feel perfectly at ease with him." [14]

That interview was the beginning of a relationship that led to the marriage on July 18, 1905, of the immigrant reporter who came from the sweatshop to the patrician reformer born of the cream of American society. What made the bridging of their social worlds possible was their apparent shared commitment to social betterment, to working directly with those on the lower rungs of the social order. Articles written by each of them during the early period of their relationship provide a sense of their outlook upon social issues. In a 1904 article entitled "Public Schools as Social Centres" J. G. Phelps Stokes, referring several times to his experience at the University Settlement, wrote of the need to transform public schools into social centers. The point was to inculcate a spirit of concern for the welfare of others, a sense of social responsibility. In what was a summary statement of the progressive view of education's role in society, Stokes wrote that "the development of the social nature is no less important than the development of the intellectual faculties. Education of the head, in disregard of the moral or social sense, leads to the grossest crimes and to the most far-reaching injustice." Selfish individual behavior was the root cause of social problems. As criminality was recognized as the product "of desire for satisfaction or gratification regardless of the injuries entailed," poverty was "in large measure due to sickness or vicious habits, but in still larger measure to inequitable industrial conditions that have been brought about through the exercise of self-centered desires for personal wealth, regardless of the interests or of the welfare of many of those engaged in its production." Individuals were responsible for wrongful social conditions, including such realities as the existence of "unhygienic environments" leading to disease and the maintenance of tenement housing. Such individualism generated "the ill-feeling and bitterness that separate people from one another, and that develop group antagonism that spread discord and disorder." Certainly in 1904 Stokes did not view class conflict as productive of social progress. What was necessary was the cultivation of a sense of "wholesome common interests" and toward that end Stokes would seek a broader use of public schools as places for community education and recreation.[15] Such a program, obviously, would greatly extend the reach of the settlement house activities in which he was already engaged.

By 1904 Stokes's work with University Settlement formed a part of a considerable record of involvement in social reform. He was active in the New York Child Labor Committee, seeking to publicize child labor abuses and to strengthen existing legislation. He was an officer of the Outdoor Recreation League and chairman of the Civic Center Committee, which sought an improved grouping of public buildings. At this time both his writings and his organizational activities reflected a reformist spirit of social uplift, not a determination to fundamentally reconstitute American society.

Rose Pastor Stokes's 1906 article, "The Condition of Working Women, from the Working Woman's Viewpoint," expressed a view rather different than that of her husband. The essential social problem she focused upon was not individual wrongdoing but rather the structural arrangements based on exploitation of labor. She observed:

> It must be perceived by even the casual observer that working women, as a rule, are permitted to retain but a portion of the value of what they produce; that they add more value to the material upon which they work than they receive in payment for their labor; that the average working woman produces, on the whole, more than she consumes, and that the excess is consumed by those who produce insufficient for their own maintenance, and who would probably resent being called working women; yet who are thus as dependent as any pauper is upon the labor of others. In other words, much of the hardship of the working classes is consequent upon the fact that they are obliged not merely to support their own families, but to contribute, whether they will or not, to the support of other families which live in idle luxury upon the products of working people's toil.

The recognition of this reality among the working people of the country, she wrote, led to "strikes and industrial disturbances, to ill-will, to class hatred, and to that craving for larger justice which underlies the socialistic program." Again she returned to the theme of exploitation, declaring that the working woman "sees no justice in an economic system which requires of one woman physical and spiritual exhaustion, in order that some other woman, absolved from the necessity of labor through the accident of birth or otherwise, may waste in idleness and luxury her product and the product of her fellows." Rose Stokes wrote here as someone who believed that class was the basic point of division in society.

In this article the need for "wholesome recreation and enjoyment" was noted, but Rose was not content with employers' efforts to provide welfare work. There was some bite in her comment that welfare secretaries were employed "to promote the social and recreational interest of working women, and comfortable reading rooms, rest rooms, social rooms, game rooms, dining rooms, and other facilities are provided . . . and the working girl is expected to duly appreciate these advantages, and to look upon the employer who provides them as a true friend of her class." But what she was concerned with was not "friendship in this narrow sense" but rather the provision of justice. Justice required fair hours of labor and fair pay for its product. Unless the woman worker felt that she received a "fair portion" of the value of her product, she could not regard as her friends those "who withhold from her the portion, however small, of that which is her due. Welfare work under such circumstances she regards as but a pacifying measure to secure her good will despite injustice or wrong, or reads into the motive of the employer the desire to improve his business by appearing before the patrons of that business as a 'fair' employer."

Rose Stokes insisted that working women had no objection to improvement of industrial conditions, but the fact remained that even with such reform the working woman "must necessarily get less than the fair reward for her labor if she receives for her day's work barely enough to hold body and soul together, while those who exploit her labor live in luxury and wastefulness, and spend in extravagant living what she has earned." And it was not only the workers that the idle classes harmed; they also injured themselves. The woman worker saw "in a vague sort of way that they who do wrong to others wrong themselves as well, because they make themselves unjust, and she can see neither rhyme nor reason in an economic system that checks tendencies toward spiritual perfection—the goal and reason for all human life."

By the time this article appeared, both Rose Pastor Stokes and her husband were moving toward affiliation with the Socialist party, but in Rose's words there was a sense of anger and indignation, born of experience, that her husband did not express. She made the main point of her piece quite clear: "Throughout the length and breadth of our land the terrible question faces our people: Shall the health and lives of our workers continue to be jeopardized and sacrificed to swell the incomes of the few? The working girl does not object to the accumulation of wealth when accumulation harms no one; but her soul cries out in revolt against the callousness and heedlessness of those who in their mad greed for gain ignore the conditions under which the gain is produced."

Rose also indicted the hypocrisy of organized Christianity. She wrote: "Particularly is it difficult for her to respect those churches in which 'uppermost seats' are bought and paid for, like so much merchandise, with money unjustly earned. The working girl who received her first Christian precepts from a hard-working mother may have a deep and abiding respect and love for Jesus and His teachings, and faith in the ultimate triumph of right, but she cannot respect that false religion mis-called Christianity, and those false teachings of its preachers, which confine themselves to blasphemously singing praises of God while re-pudiating the great commandment to 'Love thy neighbor as thyself.' "

Rose contended that workers "commonly regarded with distrust" con-tributions made to charities, "representing a few dollars spared by em-ployers from incomes wrung from human lives." But she also wrote that those who personally devoted themselves to such work were held in high esteem "and frequently warmest friendships are formed between them and working women." These last words doubtless had relevance to her relationship with Graham Stokes.

At the end of her essay Rose offered a somewhat vague statement of what was needed to remedy social conditions. She was blunt concern-ing what was wrong and unjust in society, but as yet not clear about a solution.

> More fellow-feeling is what the world most needs, more true sympathy, more determination to promote justice and right living, by being just and living right one's self; more readiness to subordinate one's personal desires in consideration of the needs of one's fellows, and of the underlying causes which occasion those needs; more of that sort of charity which leads the individual not merely to offer aid to those who suffer, but to search out and remove from human environments the needlessly harmful conditions and

the far-reaching manifestations of human greed and injustice that usually underlie the conditions to which, in last analysis, most of the suffering is due.[16]

In her unfinished autobiography Rose refers to having returned to work in a cigar factory shortly before her marriage. It was as though she was reaffirming her identity as a worker. She recalls the workers heartily congratulating her when they learned from the newspapers of the engagement of the shop girl and the millionaire. She also mentions that the Cigar Makers' union admitted her to membership, but it should be added that she and Graham visited a meeting of the union local and spoke to the workers. It was an occasion for both of them to assert their continuing involvement in labor's cause. Rose told those at the meeting: "Most of you know that I was a cigarmaker in Cleveland before I became a cigarmaker in New York. I am glad that I have had to work at a trade because it gives me an insight into the inner life of working girls. There are many things in a working girl's life that the public does not know of. In one factory where I was the workers had to sit on stools instead of on chairs, and the ten-hour day was very exhausting on the women."[17]

In his talk Graham stated his belief in trade unionism as something that was of benefit to both employers and employees. He framed the forthcoming marriage so as to imply labor's stake in the couple's happiness. "There is a great deal of injustice," he said, "in which the working people are the sufferers, and I intend to do all I can to bring about a general acknowledgement of the wrongs that exist in society, and to demonstrate the needlessness of the suffering that exists among the employees if they would only get fair play. The work in the interest of humanity that I have been carrying on I hope to carry on in a more extended way with the assistance of Miss Pastor when she is my wife, which I hope will be soon. I am glad she is a trades unionist."[18]

In the first period of their marriage, as Rose and Graham continued to live on the Lower East Side, they were each drawn into organized activities for civic betterment. Graham became involved with William Randolph Hearst's Municipal Ownership League. Hearst, the multi-millionaire newspaper publisher, established this New York variant of "gas and water" socialism as a personal venture.[19] Rose worked at the University Settlement but also became an activist in the Charity Organization Society. By the early 1900s this group was based on growing cooperation between settlement workers and those involved in providing charity to the needy.[20]

By the middle of 1906, however, liberal reform, mixed with a flavoring of upper-class noblesse oblige, was not enough for Rose Pastor Stokes, and in this she was joined by her husband. They entered a period of intense, well-publicized activity as members of the Socialist party and the Intercollegiate Socialist Society, an independent organization dedicated to furthering serious discussion of socialist ideas, especially within the academic community. Rose was in considerable demand as a platform speaker, whose working-class experience imparted a passionate authenticity to her socialist views. Graham became the president of the I.S.S. In that period, as Rose writes, she regarded her husband as an informed and thoughtful representative of socialist thought.

In his autobiography the artist Rockwell Kent gave his recollection of Rose and Graham Stokes during their years of socialist activism. Kent remembers calling Graham Stokes "the brotherly spirit of socialism"; Graham was "ever courageous to the limits of his understanding, he was a Christlike man." But Rose was "imbued with passion" and through that passion "with a far deeper understanding." For a time Kent and his wife Kathleen were guests at the Stokes home on Caritas Island, near Stamford, Connecticut. A stream of radical intellectuals made their way to Caritas for visits of longer or shorter duration. Kent candidly writes that both Rose and Graham "were as spiritually disembodied and generally impractical a pair as one might ever meet." The couple had ardently desired a child, but Kent recalls poet Horace Traubel's comment that "the trouble is, they don't know how to go about it."[21] The Stokeses were deeply involved in the realities of the social struggle but there was an otherworldliness about their own relationship.

A 1910 *New York Times* interview with Graham Stokes provided a sense of his conception of the socialist movement. As the newspaper frankly stated, the basic reason for the interview was the apprehension that socialism had become a serious matter in the United States. The interviewer reported that it was likely the election results that year "would give us conservatives cold chills." What was there then to this movement? For an answer he would turn to "the most interesting Socialist in America," James Graham Phelps Stokes. What above all made Graham Stokes interesting was his marriage. The union was evidence of democracy in American life. The interviewer, Edward Marshall, wrote: "Mr. Stokes is the hero of our greatest social romance, a figure in the one marriage of recent years that has come nearer than any other to demonstrating the ideal of universal brotherhood. Member of a Church of England family of the most orthodox type and austere traditions, he chose for his wife, a few years ago, a Jewish cigarette girl, Rose Pastor."

When asked if he saw evidence of anything to give hope to socialists, Stokes emphasized the growing receptivity to socialist ideas found among journalists. More and more editors were "doing what they can to admit socialistic articles and arguments into their columns."

Stokes saw the profits received by capitalists as a modern counterpart to the unjust taxation imposed upon the American colonists by King George. He did not advocate recompense for past wrongs, but the robbery would now have to end. Stokes explained he did not desire violent revolution, but he did declare that "if violent revolt comes, when the exploiters of the people attempt by force to compel the continued payment of unearned tribute to them, then such violent revolt against violence will be justified." The only hope for peaceful change that Stokes saw was "the arousing of public opinion of such strength that the ruling class would be compelled to "permit continuing limitations of their opportunities, until unearned profit-taking shall no longer be a possibility." In

1910 Stokes was of the opinion that reform movements, "honest administration of public affairs," were commendable but they were definitely not enough.[22]

Rose Pastor Stokes shared with her husband a commitment to publicizing the cause of socialism. But unlike Graham, she also was drawn to labor's immediate struggles and eagerly supported several important strikes. She played a part in the memorable 1909 shirtwaist-makers' strike in New York. More than twenty thousand workers had walked out of hundreds of shops in Manhattan and Brooklyn. This strike was an occasion in which socialists, suffragists, and liberals from the Women's Trade Union League were able to cooperate in support of the strikers. Rose spoke at several public gatherings to rally public support. This struggle, involving thousands in an industry-wide strike, resulted in victory, and she doubtless took satisfaction that she was involved in securing better working and living conditions for the garment workers.

A reporter for the *New York Times* noted that Rose Pastor Stokes's association with the strike drew the particular interest of journalists and news illustrators. It was clear that the *Times* staffer had a favorable view of Rose's personality and was moved by her life's story. There was a rather full account of her appearance:

> Mrs. Stokes is small and slight. Were her face less young looking or her movements less long and quick, her thinness would be unpleasant, but, combined as it is with the youth and the dash, it merely gives a boyish look that is oddly pleasant to her figure. She stoops her shoulders. Her face is long and narrow, and looks more so than it actually is because she wears her hair parted and drawn loosely down into a braided knot at the nape of her neck. With curious perfection do her eyes and hair match. Both are a rather light but very live shade of brown, and they appear almost vivid against the heavy white of her complexion. Her face, as a whole, is sweet and appealing.

She gave the press an outline of her earlier years as a shop worker in Cleveland and mentioned that on a pay of six to eight dollars she was the main support of the Pastor family. A journalist asked: "You had to take care of eight people on $8 a week?" Rose reportedly nodded her head and replied, "Yes, my dear." The *Times* correspondent wrote that she was "immensely effective" as a speaker, and indeed her life was "practically migratory" for the cause. It was perhaps almost incomprehensible that now married to a husband of wealth she did not choose a more leisured life. But there was an explanation. "Perhaps the look which came over her features as she recalled those very years may explain her attitude now. Any experiences strong enough to throw such an expression on a person's face are also strong enough, perhaps, to spur that person on to try to remove the probability of their occurring to others." The reporter found her "absolutely unaffected . . . intangible, illusive, charming," but she was also a person of serious ideas. At the end of the interview she said: "My ideal is that we all be economically interdependent. We should not be independent like millionaires, nor dependent like laborers. My ideal is that we all be interdependent." And she announced that she was not working in a losing cause.[23]

She was also in the thick of the action in the 1912 hotel workers' strike. This job action, led by the International Hotel Workers' Union, was a protest against the bitterly oppressive labor conditions prevailing in New York's hotels. Workers at such major hotels as the Plaza and the old Waldorf-Astoria and at Churchill's, Delmonico's, and Sherry's restaurants participated in the walkout. With the backing of the Industrial Workers of the World (IWW), the strike was organized along lines of industrial unionism, and Rose saw an important principle of working-class solidarity at issue in the struggle. Along with IWW figures Joseph Ettor and Arturo Giovannitti, she addressed large crowds gathered to support the strikers. She was not content, however, with speechmaking and immersed herself in the actual organizational work of the strikers. She was particularly active in efforts to enlist the support of the chambermaids, and joined by black socialist Hubert H. Harrison took part in a meeting to organize black waiters.[24]

Rose's role in this strike brought her some criticism, including the comment of her husband's uncle, W. E. D. Stokes, that she was "up-setting the minds of thousands of waiters, busses and cooks who came here from distant lands, some, perhaps, with the honest intention of becoming good American citizens."[25] Only when pressure mounted for the workers to accept the employers' compromise offer did she resign from the executive board of the union. The settlement brought concessions in hours and wages, but the union did not achieve recognition as the workers' collective bargaining agent. Within months the hotel workers were again on strike, in an even more bitter struggle for better conditions.

Rose's attention was also engaged by the legendary 1913 Paterson silk workers' strike. This time she used her literary talents, contributing a poem to the cause:

> Our folded hands again are at the loom.
>> The air
> Is ominous with peace.
> But what we weave you see not through the gloom.
> 'Tis terrible with doom.
>> Beware!
>
> You dream that we are weaving what you will?
>> Take care!
> Our fingers do not cease:
> We've starved—and lost, but we are weavers still;
> And Hunger's in the mill!
>
> And Hunger moves the shuttle forth and back.
>> Take care!
> The product grows and grows . . .
> A shroud it is; a shroud of ghastly black.
> We've never let you lack!
>> Beware!
>
> The Warp and Woof of Misery and Defeat
>> Take care!
> See how the shuttle goes!

Our braised hearts with bitter hopes now beat:
The shuttle's sure—and fleet![26]

Rose Pastor Stokes's relation to the Paterson strike also extended to the defense of Patrick Quinlan, an IWW strike activist sentenced to prison for incitement to riot. In conjunction with the Free Speech League, the most well-known civil libertarian organization of the pre-World War I era, she actively sought support for Quinlan's release. She was steadfast in her commitment to this cause, but Quinlan was released in November 1916 only after having served his term.

In 1915 Rose became involved with the birth control movement, joining the National Birth Control League. At this time, according to Linda Gordon, women's socialist groups and IWW locals were mainly responsible for birth control agitation.[27] Rose Pastor Stokes's enlistment in the struggle was fully in accord with her socialism. Early in 1916, on the eve of Margaret Sanger's trial in New York on charges of distributing birth control information in violation of the Comstock Act, Rose served as master of ceremonies at a Brevoort Hotel dinner honoring Sanger. Among those attending were John Reed, Walter Lippmann, and Kate Hepburn, pioneer suffragist and mother of actress Katherine Hepburn.[28]

Stokes's participation in the movement was highlighted by her platform appearance at a May 5, 1916, Carnegie Hall rally marking Emma Goldman's release from jail after serving a short sentence for distributing birth control information. Rose's interval at the podium followed speeches by Arturo Giovannitti, Max Eastman, and Leonard D. Abbott. Her speech was an indictment of bourgeois hypocrisy, for the rich had access to means of contraception, while the poor were denied the information that could be used to regulate family size. She related the birth control movement as an immediate social struggle to the long-term goal of socialism. Short of socialism that would produce basic societal changes there were "lesser causes . . . worth fighting for, and birth control is such a cause."[29]

At this gathering Rose was not content to deliver a speech. At the conclusion of her remarks she announced that she had with her slips of paper outlining birth control procedures. She told the audience: "Capitalist society has not succeeded in making me bitter, but it has succeeded in making me unafraid. Therefore, be the penalty what it may, I here frankly offer to give out these slips with the forbidden information to those needy wives and mothers who will frankly come and take them." [30] The crowd rushed to take the proffered information and a near riot ensued. Rose escaped unharmed and waited for the expected arrest for having incited disorder. But, perhaps because of the Stokeses' elevated social position, there would be no arrest. Stokes was unhappy about this class discrimination; and, regarding her special role in the movement, activist Jessie Ashley wrote her: "they think you *want* to be arrested and they are loath to increase the notoriety of the b.c. propaganda. They think your trial would be as widely advertised as Margaret Sanger's or Emma Goldman's. In any case it seems to me to the advantage of all of us to keep you out of jail. While you are free you can go about doing your work." [31] It may also be there was a reluctance to create in the public's eye a too close association of birth control with socialism.

Rose Pastor Stokes's role at the Carnegie Hall meeting brought reproaches from the Stokes family. Polite discourse, even for the purpose of articulating radical views, was one thing, but for the Stokeses the Carnegie Hall scene smacked of rowdyism. Anson Phelps Stokes wrote to Rose at some length, explaining his position that defiance of law and order was wrong. He hoped she would apologize for her defiance of the police and indicate she had been misquoted in the press. But Rose insisted she had done nothing that required apology or retraction. She wrote her brother-in-law: "I was neither defiant, nor bitter, nor unwilling to pay the penalty." What she did at Carnegie Hall was done because she believed "the act would cause a country-wide discussion of the problem . . . and make millions of women, unaware heretofore, aware of the existence of such a thing as Birth Control." [32] She believed the Comstock Law was vicious and she wanted that point driven home by its enforcement in her case.

Parallel to her activism Stokes sought expression through the medium of the theater, contributing a play, *The Woman Who Wouldn't,* focused on the theme of a woman's independence. In a work of considerable power she brought to life the process of self-actualization that took the working-class flower maker Mary to a position as acknowledged champion of workers. The kernel of the drama is Mary's refusal to engage in a loveless marriage even for the usually adequate reason of providing a father for her unborn child. The play portrays the anguish but also the triumph that comes from leading a life of principle. Mary's child is to become one of the "women of tomorrow," and it is most likely that Stokes saw herself as such a woman. In this play Stokes merges her socialist commitment with an eloquent feminism.[33]

The tumultuous year of 1917, the year of American entrance into the World War and of the Russian Revolution, marked a fork in the road for Rose Pastor Stokes. A few months before the Wilson administration's decision for war she declined on behalf of herself and Graham an invitation to attend a peace demonstration at Washington Square.[34] As explained in her autobiographical manuscript her initial response to the outbreak of war was to endorse the Wilson policies, moving in step with her husband. In the summer of 1917 she was listed as one of the contributing members of the Vigilantes, a pro-war group.[35] In May she was one of a group of pro-war socialists who cabled European socialists calling for bringing the war to a quick end through the overthrow of "kaiserism."[36] Due to her participation in a variety of activities in support of the war effort, it might have been imagined that Stokes was making the transition from radicalism to Establishment liberalism.

The climax of Stokes's support of the war came with publication of her article "A Confession" in the December 1917 issue of the *Century* magazine. She acknowledged that previously she had held the United States to be among the most oppressive of nations. "I have always repudiated America," she wrote. But now she had come to recognize "that the monster which oppresses equally the American citizen and the alien immigrant is not America, but capitalism, peculiar to no country, eating at the heart of each—citizen sinister of the world." America, she now knew, stood among the free nations of the world, "eager to follow where Liberty beckons, eager to fight for a newer, better world, burning to strike a blow at Injustice and Oppression wherever these may raise their heads, whether they appear in the guise of German autocracy abroad or special privilege at home." Earlier she had viewed nationalism as contradictory to internationalism, but now she understood this was "an absolutely fictitious doctrine, and one that the socialist movement, if it would be true to its own principles, must at once discard." Internationalism had made a nationalist of her and when President Wilson "uttered the great watchword of the struggle—the word that sent a thrill through the very heart of every democratic nation in the world," she became an American. She clearly continued to see herself as a socialist and indeed equated the war against Germany with union labor's struggle against scabs. At the end of the piece she provided a poem, "America," celebrating the American soldiers who marched to battle "wearing the uniform of world-democracy."[37] In this cause she was ready to give her all to America. For a moment in history Rose Pastor Stokes had embraced the Wilsonian view of the world struggle.

The moment, however, did not last long. Something of what ensued was due, as she later recalled, to her disillusionment with the National party, a conglomeration, lacking a labor base, of ex-socialists and other assorted personalities, that disintegrated almost as quickly as it was organized.[38] Crucial was the Bolshevik Revolution of November 1917, which set her on a new political path from which she would never swerve. In the fall of 1917, although still holding to her support of Wilson's policies, she endorsed Morris Hillquit, the Socialist party's candidate for mayor of New York City. In December she wrote privately that she saw no way of equalizing the burden of the world "except by the action of the peoples of all countries who seek to establish social and industrial democracy." The Russians, she observed, were the only people who seemed to be "moving rapidly in that direction, garbled and twisted as the reports may be that come to us through the capitalist press out of that wonderful country."[39] Only in revolution was hope to be found. In February 1918 she returned to the Socialist party.

Once having settled upon her view of events, Rose Pastor Stokes was not one to be content with private dissent. In March 1918 she left New York on a speaking tour of the Midwest. In Kansas City, Missouri, she ran into serious trouble, encountering the force of the wartime hysteria. In a speech to the Woman's Dining Club she denounced war and capitalism. If there was any doubt as to her position she set the record straight when the *Kansas City Star* reported she had claimed to both support the government and oppose the war. In a letter to the editor she declared: "No government which is *for* the profiteers can also be for the people, and I am *for* the people, while the government is for the profiteers." On March 23 she was arrested by federal agents and charged with violation of the Espionage Act. This wartime measure provided for censorship of the press, gave the administration wide powers to exclude publications from the mails, and provided severe penalties for anyone who made "false reports or false statements with intent to interfere with the operation or success of the military or naval forces of the United States or to promote the success of its enemies" or who sought to cause refusal of duty in the armed forces or obstructed military recruitment.[40] The law furnished a means of stifling and branding as espionage speech that the government found offensive. Although Graham Stokes came to Kansas City to arrange bail for his wife he left her to face the trial alone.

The trial of Rose Pastor Stokes for violation of all three clauses of Title I, Section 3 of the Espionage Act began on May 21, 1918. Stokes's defense attorneys were Seymour Stedman and Harry Sullivan; the former, referred to derisively and pointedly by the prosecution as the "socialist lawyer," would in September 1918 serve as chief counsel in the Espionage Act trial of Eugene V. Debs. The United States District Attorney, Francis M. Wilson, and his assistant, Elmer B. Silvers, acted on behalf of the government. The trial was presided over by United States District Judge Arba S. Van Valkenburgh.

The prosecution's case was essentially this: To bear the burden of proof that Rose Pastor Stokes intended to make "false statements" in order to interfere with the success of American military forces, to cause "refusal of duty," and to "obstruct" the enlistment or recruitment services of the United States, it offered a parade of witnesses who testified to the content of the Woman's Dining Club speech. According to their version of Stokes's two-hour lecture, the invited speaker had charged that American soldiers were not in the war "to save the world for democracy," but to save the loans extended to the Allies by J. P. Morgan, and that if we were "sincere" in our professed democratic crusade, we would have entered the conflagration when the "neutrality of Belgium had been violated" or when the *Lusitania* had been torpedoed. Stokes had also said that she was sorry that she had written a patriotic poem after witnessing young American boys marching on Fifth Avenue in New York City, and that when they came home from the trenches on the Western front, this country would be plunged into revolution. She had praised the Bolsheviks, argued that the work of the Red Cross was "mere war camouflage," and spoke well of Emma Goldman.[41]

There was further testimony about a second Stokes speech made on March 20, 1918, in Neosho, Missouri, in which she was reputed to have stated that while President Wilson was "honest and sincere," his administration was "controlled absolutely by the moneyed class," and that "she couldn't advise nor urge men to fight in this war for the reason that it was for the profiteers" (154–55). James N. Purcell, Chief Deputy United States Marshal, called to the stand, testified that in a conversation after her arrest, Stokes had repeated her accusation that the government was controlled by the profiteers, and had said that it made no difference to working people which side won (158–60). S. W. Dillingham of the Bureau of Investigation, who had participated in the arrest, had asked Stokes whether it was her objective to "cause a revolution in this country, as in Russia," and she had answered succinctly in the affirmative (163–64). A reporter for the *Kansas City Post* who had spoken with Mrs. Stokes in the courtroom prior to her arraignment, stated that she had said that the people had become "war crazy," that the profiteers had obtained a stranglehold over the government, and that she feared for the "working people whose conditions were already so bad" (126–29). And finally there was testimony from an Army captain, stationed at Camp Funston, Kansas, that the March 20, 1918, issue of the *Kansas City Star* had been circulated at the base and that he had seen, read, and commented upon the contents of her communication (173–74).

To neutralize this testimony, Stedman called a series of witnesses who had attended the meeting of the Woman's Dining Club, had heard the Stokes speech, and who denied that she had referred to the Red Cross as "mere war camouflage," that she expressed regrets about the war poem she had authored, and that she argued that the "saving the world for democracy" slogan was a subterfuge to induce young men to enlist in the armed forces (247–73). Florence Allen, the nation's foremost proponent of state labor legislation to protect women in the workplace, and a visitor to Kansas City for a meeting of the National Conference of Social Work, testified that she had known Rose Pastor Stokes for ten years, and that her friend's general reputation as a law-abiding citizen was good (176–78). And Stokes herself on the witness stand explained the framework and contents of her Dining Club speech, quoted statistics from the report of the Chairman of the War Finance Committee demonstrating the extraordinary increase in wartime profits made by American corporations, and read excerpts from Woodrow Wilson's *The New Freedom* into the record to show that the president himself had once accused American entrepreneurs of controlling the government: "Page 25. I speak . . . of the control of the government exercised by Big Business . . . . Page 35. The government which was designed for the people, has got into the hands of bosses and their employers, the special interests. An invisible empire has been set up above the forms of democracy" (180–214).

But to no avail. At the conclusion of the testimony, after Stedman's motion for a directed verdict had been overruled, Francis Wilson made his closing statement. Rose Pastor Stokes was a "foreign woman," "the most vicious German propagandist in the United States of America," "a frenzied fanatic upon Socialism." In her speech before the Woman's Dining Club she schemed to inject the "poison" of sedition among her listeners "so that it may spread as a pestilence" and interfere with the success of America's military forces, foment mutiny and refusal of duty and obstruct the enlistment and recruitment services. She had a "vicious" heart, filled with hatred for America, and she wanted to precipitate a Bolshevik-style revolution in which land would be confiscated and the wealth of those men who have been "active and energetic and who have fought their way in the world" would be expropriated and distributed among the masses (293–307).

Whatever drama the district attorney's histrionics injected into the trial and however persuasive his closing statement might have been to the jury, the instructions of Judge Van Valkenburgh were more important. Van Valkenburgh's charge to the jury epitomized the "war hysteria" of the federal judiciary that Supreme Court Justice Oliver Wendell Holmes, Jr., privately deplored a year later. "Now, gentlemen of the jury," the federal judge said, "the newspaper in which the publication was made reaches a great number of people even in the Army camps of the United States."

> Among those outside such camps are men within the age of enlistment, to wit, between the ages of 18–45, and within the age of conscription, to wit, between the ages of 21 and 30 years. There are those who have already registered and received their serial numbers as a preliminary to entrance upon active service in the Army and Navy of the United States; there are the mothers, fathers, wives, sisters, brothers, sweethearts and friends of these men . . . If the statement made in this letter and the resulting attitude therein voiced should meet with credence and acceptance by any appreciable number of its readers, could they fail to produce a temper and spirit that would interfere and tend naturally and logically to interfere with the operation and success of the military and naval forces of the United States. (311)

Van Valkenburgh was certain that the free speech clause of the First Amendment did not protect the contents of the Stokes letter to the

Kansas City Star. "This prosecution," he declared, "in no wise invades the constitutional right of free speech and free press. . . . Honest criticism made in the interest of the government and intended to favor and forward the policies to which it is committed, and to which all loyal citizens owe adhesion, is no offense; but words and acts hostile to these policies and intended to paralyze and defeat the efforts of government do not come within that category and . . . cannot be permitted"(319).

On May 23, 1918, with these instructions, the fathers and brothers and friends who composed the jury began their deliberations. They returned five hours later at 7:30 P.M.: Rose Pastor Stokes was found guilty on all three counts of the indictment. According to her male peers, she had interfered with the success of the United States in the war, counseled refusal of duty, and obstructed the recruitment and enlistment services. On June 1, after the ritualistic motions for a new trial and arrest of judgment were denied, after Stokes stated that she had taken "the provisions of the Constitution concerning liberty of expression too literally, language plain and simple and made a part of the Constitution by an amendment thereto by those who recognized its importance during periods not all of peace but also of stress"(353), and after Van Valkenburgh responded by condemning "the defiance of the popular will" and analogized the defendant's crimes to an "organic disease which involves the whole body politic and threatens the health and very life of the entire nation"(355), Stokes was sentenced to ten years of imprisonment in the Missouri State Penitentiary. The defense attorneys immediately filed a petition for the writ of error to the United States Court of Appeals for the Eighth Circuit.

The sentencing of Rose Pastor Stokes came one day after Senator William Borah rose to address his fellow senators on the question of war profiteering to which Stokes had referred in Kansas City. Borah introduced a resolution directing the secretary of the treasury to furnish information concerning such profiteering, and in the course of his remarks he reminded his colleagues that "a few days ago a noted woman in this country with whose methods as to government most of us disagree, but with whose humanitarian objects and purposes many of us agree, was convicted in an American court." He quoted the words of Stokes's *Kansas City Star* letter, "No government which is for the profiteers can also be for the people," and observed, "Nothing is truer than that statement." If the government had the facts regarding profiteering but refused to take appropriate action, the government, Borah declared, "is derelict and justly subject to the criticism of everybody who is for the people." In the event the president informed the Congress and the American people of the facts and no action was taken, Rose Pastor Stokes, he said, "will no longer be a criminal, but a martyr." He noted additionally: "Now, a government may close the lips of an individual; you may reduce them all to silence for a time; but every time you close the lips of an individual and fail to remedy the wrong you put a thousand more to thinking, and you can not prevent people from thinking."[42]

Two weeks later, on June 14, 1918, President Wilson wrote to Attorney General Thomas Gregory that the Stokes verdict was "very just" and asked whether it would be possible to indict the managing editor of the *Kansas City Star* for having printed her letter in the newspaper.[43] But not all members of the Wilson administration agreed with the president's assessment. Alfred Bettman, assistant to the attorney general, expressed "considerable doubt" that the Stokes case, "having arisen before the amendment of the Espionage Act" on May 16, 1918, came within the terms of the law. "The case has been argued," he wrote on February 10, 1919, "before the Circuit Court of Appeals. In the event of an affirmance, questions of reduction of sentence would come up. The ten year sentence was . . . ridiculously excessive."[44]

Rose Pastor Stokes was professedly not concerned about the length of her sentence. "I maintain," she argued on July 6, 1918, "that we have the right to express honest opinions and convictions—that minorities should have the right in war or in peace, to oppose the majority in power, and on any issues that seem to them vital and necessary. . . . I have no fear of a prison sentence long or short."[45] In the brief submitted to the Eighth Circuit Court of Appeals, along with more technical arguments, Stedman, Sullivan, and Isaac Edward Ferguson invoked the protections of the First Amendment. "Our Constitution was written under the profound inspiration of the theory of natural rights. It was written with great jealousy of the encroachments of the power of government on the liberties of the individual and the scruple was to give the individual the largest possible freedom from governmental interference. . . . It is for the courts to be the haven of treasured liberties."[46]

In January 1920 the Eighth Circuit in an opinion by Judge Sanborn reversed the conviction of Rose Pastor Stokes and remanded for a new trial. "The trial," wrote Sanborn, "was in the midst of . . . war when patriotic men were particularly impatient of every interference and of every attempt to interfere with or cripple the universal efforts to win that war." In these circumstances, "extraordinary coolness, calm and impartiality were indispensable." But Judge Van Valkenburgh was not impartial. His instructions to the jury contained "rich, inspiring expressions of patriotism and of the nobility of our aims in the war." Yet his "patriotic zeal" placed "too heavy a burden upon the defendant in her endeavor to meet the evidence which the government produced against her."[47] A year later the Harding administration, loath to bring Rose Pastor Stokes to trial again, *nulle prossed* the case.

Wilsonian rhetoric about global freedom had been accompanied by willingness to extinguish constitutional liberty at home. In 1919 the antiwar Socialist Kate Richards O'Hare, who was imprisoned for alleged violation of the Espionage Act, observed: "How shriekingly funny is all the wild hullabaloo about the 'profiteers,' and poor Rose Pastor Stokes got ten years for mildly suggesting that there were such animals in a most ladylike little note."[48]

During the months after her conviction Stokes rallied to the defense of Eugene V. Debs, initially charged with violation of ten of the twelve clauses of the Espionage Act as modified by the amendments of May 16, 1918 (commonly known as the Sedition Act). As Debs went on trial in Cleveland, Stokes was at his side in the courtroom. In his address to the jury the socialist leader said: "Why think of sentencing women like Rose Pastor Stokes and Kate Richards O'Hare to the penitentiary? These women have consecrated their lives to the suffering, struggling poor. In a true civilization they would be given places of honor and citizens would revere them for their works and call them blessed." He said of Stokes: "Throughout all her life she has been on the side of the oppressed and downtrodden. If she were so inclined she might occupy a place of ease. She might enjoy all of the comforts and leisures of life. Instead of this, she has renounced them all. She has taken her place among the poor, and there she has worked with all of her ability, all of her energy, to make it possible for them to enjoy a little more of the comforts of life."[49] Debs was also convicted and sentenced to ten years, and in his case there would be no overturning of the verdict. To the directors of American official policy, it was symbolically important that the leading symbol of opposition to the war go to jail.

Prior to the war, Debs had viewed Rose Pastor Stokes as a valued friend and, as Ray Ginger notes, he had not denounced her even when she was among the war supporters, for he believed in her sincerity and dedication to principle.[50] He remained steadfast in his friendly attitude, at one point writing Rose: "Not one day passes but our blessing goes out to you over the invisible wires . . . we love you with all our hearts and trust you with our honor and our lives." Even in the mid 1920s when differences over the significance of Bolshevism came to the fore, Debs wrote Rose that "the time will come when we will again stand beneath the same banner as we have in the past."[51]

As the Socialist party divided in response to the emergence of Soviet Russia, Rose Pastor Stokes joined with the left-wingers who saw Leninism as the path to the future. In 1919 at Chicago she participated in the first convention of the Communist party and established a political direction for herself that would continue to the end of her life. She had found an enduring political home, but the commitments inspired by war and revolution led to the dissolution of her marriage. For Graham Stokes the period of involvement with radical activism had come to a definite end. Breaking with the Socialist party over the war, he became strongly anticommunist in political outlook. In February 1919 he wrote a letter to the *New York Times*, claiming that the Soviet regime had secretly committed enormous sums of money for a secret propaganda campaign aiming at the overthrow of the U.S. government. Such radicals as John Reed and Albert Rhys Williams were to be viewed as extensions of this conspiratorial Soviet effort. Later that year, again in the *Times*, he wrote a piece commending the credentials of Admiral Kolchak, one of the Russian counterrevolutionaries seeking the overthrow of the Lenin government. He emphasized that Kolchak's bodyguard on one tour of the Siberian front consisted of a hundred British troops led by one Colonel John Ward, who had previously been an official of the General Federation of Trades Unions in Great Britain. Kolchak, as Stokes presented him, was the champion of law and order who would combat both the Left and Right. Such, he said, was the man who sought "recognition and aid of all who love democracy."[52]

The political differences between Rose Pastor Stokes and her husband became personal ones as well. Graham vehemently objected to Rose's welcoming to their home persons he viewed as "ingrate enemies" of America.[53] "You ask me to return," she wrote to Graham, February 18, 1925: "That I went ultimately is due, not to a fit of temper or of mean disregard for your feelings . . . but for the most profound conviction that even the kind of armed truce that existed between us at the house was impossible to maintain because of the deep-going fundamental difference in our aims, our ideals, our principles and convictions."[54] Divorce came in 1925. In 1926, in an article for *Collier's*, she argued for a liberalization of divorce laws. She may have had her relationship with Stokes in mind when she wrote: "Among the wealthy most men are victims of business, most women victims of business men. The man whose soul is daily absorbed in the game of making profits or driving hard bargains cannot long retain the spiritual and emotional qualities necessary to a real lover."[55] In 1927 Rose Pastor Stokes married Jerome Romain, who later, as V. J. Jerome, became a prominent communist theoretician and editor.

For several years Rose served as a member of the Central Executive Committee of the Workers party, the legal extension of the Communist party that had been driven underground by the Red scare. She was one of those arrested for having taken part in a Communist party convention, held at Bridgman, Michigan, in 1922, but her case was never brought to trial. In 1921 she was secretary of the women's division of the Friends of Soviet Russia and was especially active in organizing famine relief urgently needed by the Soviets in the aftermath of the bitter civil war years. For a time she headed the women's work department of the Workers party and urged special attention to the organizing of working-class women. The married working-class woman, she wrote, "the mere slave of a poor wage slave . . . bears within her agonized soul the seed of revolt."[56] The revolutionaries must make possible the flowering of that seed.

On the international scene Rose Pastor Stokes played a significant role at the Fourth Congress of the Communist International, held in Moscow during November–December 1922. Along with two black American representatives, Otto Huiswood and poet Claude McKay, she took part in the deliberations of the Negro Commission of the Congress. The product of these discussions was the adoption of a declaration stating that "the Fourth Congress recognizes the necessity of supporting every form of Negro Movement which tends to undermine or weaken capitalism or imperialism or to impede its further penetration." The Communist International pledged to fight "for race equality of the Negro with the white people, for equal wages and political and social rights." Communists were to "exert every effort" on behalf of admitting blacks to trade unions.

It was Rose Pastor Stokes who presented the "Thesis on the Negro Question" to the Congress for adoption. The thesis argued that the whole sweep of their history prepared American blacks "for an important role in the liberation struggle of the entire African race." Reference was made to the cruel oppression of slavery, but blacks had not merely been passive victims: "The Negro was no docile slave. He rebelled. His

history is rich in rebellion, insurrection, underground methods of securing liberty, but his struggles were barbarously crushed. He was tortured
into submission and the bourgeois press and religion justified his slavery."
When chattel slavery clashed with advancing capitalism, slavery had to
go, but the Civil War "left the Negro the choice of peonage in the South
or wage slavery in the North." Events since the World War, "post-war
industrialization of the Negro in the North and the spirit of revolt en-
gendered by post-war persecutions and brutalities" had created a new
situation placing blacks "in the vanguard of the African struggle against
oppression." The nub of the resolution was the statement that what
was called the "Negro problem" had become "a vital question of the
world revolution." As was also the case with Asian peoples cooperation
with "our oppressed black fellow men" was to be understood as essential to the revolutionary cause.[57] The formulations Rose Pastor Stokes
outlined signified a decisive break with the old Socialist party view of
the racial question as not requiring any special struggle for black rights.
The situation of American blacks was moved toward the top of the communist agenda. As Theodore Draper writes, the document drafted by
the Fourth Congress "represents the first real effort of the Comintern to
formulate a position on the Negro question and deserves more attention
than it has received."[58]

In the course of the Comintern discussion Stokes emphasized aspects of the question that were not reflected in the final resolution. She
took up the matter of race consciousness and argued that Communists
had "nothing to fear in any surviving race consciousness in the darker
workers who join us in the revolutionary struggle in the proletarian
field." After all, she noted, where color, "by universal bourgeois dogma
becomes a badge of inferiority, a man of color is not permitted to forget
it." At the same time she insisted that white Communists, "especially
those who are to make contact with the Negro Communist groups—
get the bourgeois color psychosis completely, as it is now only partially,
uprooted from their systems."[59] She brought a considerable degree of
sophistication to her view of the American racial scene.

Rose Pastor Stokes was not to have a long life. Involved in the late 1920s with personal problems, she was less politically active than previously but she never turned away from the path she had chosen. In 1930 she commented that the very existence of the Communist party gave her zest for living. That year she developed cancer, which would not yield to surgery and which would only temporarily go into remission. She bravely fought the disease and went to Germany for radiation treatment. In New York, on April 15, 1933, some five hundred persons gathered to honor Rose Pastor Stokes and to raise funds for her medical treatment. Marxist publisher Alexander Trachtenberg presided and such veterans of the radical movements as Leonard Abbott, Richard B. Moore, Michael Gold, and Anna Strunsky Walling spoke.[60] Some weeks earlier, in a shaky, weakened hand, Rose Pastor Stokes wrote Maximillian Cohen that she was "very ill . . . very lonely—but fighting."[61] Her fight ended on June 20, in a Germany ruled by Adolph Hitler. She had lived a life of fidelity to principles in which she believed and of loyalty to the oppressed from whom she had come. Commitment, for her, was not some affectation or intellectual rationalization but rather the natural, honest expression of what she was. She embodied what she once said were Walt Whitman's greatest qualities, a willingness to voice one's thoughts in the face of bitterest opposition and the courage not to be restrained by convention from sympathy with the fallen.[62]

• • •

The manuscript presented here is the unfinished autobiography that Rose Pastor Stokes undertook to write during the period of her final illness. Two versions of the autobiography exist. One is that included in the Rose Pastor Stokes Papers, deposited at Yale University. The other, a considerably longer manuscript, is found in the V. J. Jerome collection, also at Yale. According to Patrick Renshaw the shorter version had been rewritten "to conform with changes in the positions of the Communist party to which Rose belonged for the last dozen years or so of her life."[63] This hypothesis ignores the probability that Rose Pastor Stokes, at the end of her life, on the basis of considered judgment, sought to emphasize her devotion to the Communist party. Her desire to do this may have had no relation whatever to changes in the party's positions. In any event the version now published is the longer and more nearly complete "Jerome" manuscript.

Before her death Stokes had contacted Samuel Ornitz, Hollywood screenwriter and novelist (in 1947, one of the Hollywood Ten, subpoenaed by the House Committee on Un-American Activities), informing him that the autobiography was almost completed, but that because of her ill health, she would not be able to finish the last quarter of the book. She hoped that Ornitz would be able to write the remaining chapters as "biography" and that they would cover the period "from the time of the Proletarian Revolution; my return to the Socialist Party, my trip to Kansas City, my speech, the letter to the *Star,* the indictment, trial etc. . . . Then the left wing developing in the Socialist Party and the organization of the Communist Party and beyond that more intimate personal history." "I long to see," she wrote on her typewriter, "the book out by spring. My feeling is that if I don't succeed in making it a Spring publication of 1933, I'll never see it off the press."[64]

Ornitz was a logical choice as the writer who would complete the autobiography and attend to its publication. Apart from his left-wing political orientation, he had demonstrated in his novel, *Haunch Paunch and Jowl,* a sophisticated, sensitive account of the East Side immigrant experience from which Rose Pastor Stokes emerged. Providing as context for the book a vivid portrayal of the poverty and despair afflicting the ghetto Jews, Ornitz created as his central character a symbol of overweening ambition and opportunism. Meyer Hirsch, driven by his desire for material success and respectability, schemes and calculates his way up the social ladder, advances to a lucrative career as lawyer, and then achieves the goal of becoming a judge on the bench of the Superior Criminal Court.

The heart of the novel, then, is the theme of the transformation of the upwardly striving immigrant youth into the typification of the American bourgeois, the *allrightnik,* smug and content with things as they are.

But there is also a related theme of unrequited, unfulfilled love, Hirsch's yearning for Esther Brinn, a young woman of principle, refinement, and culture. At the age of sixteen Esther "was but a slight, growing girl" but later she "sprang out of the chrysalis of the awkward age and dazzled our whole beings with her exquisite beauty." As the novel moves toward its conclusion Hirsch is overwhelmed with the news that Esther Brinn has married Barney Finn, the Yankee settlement house worker who ardently seeks political reform and is also fortunate enough to inherit several millions of dollars. The newspapers report the marriage with such head-lines as "Poor Jewish Girl Marries Millionaire Sociologist." Esther Brinn and Barney Finn are clearly patterned after Rose Pastor Stokes and her husband Graham. Esther Brinn is a figure of memorable depth and in-tegrity, and Samuel Ornitz leaves no doubt that he shared the contempt that Rose felt for the conventional life of careerism and equivocation. In terms of how Ornitz would present her life's story to the reading audi-ence, Rose Pastor Stokes had good reason to believe she could rely upon the author's understanding of the lofty aspirations she had striven to realize.[65]

In June 1933, after Stokes's death, Marguerite Young, in an article in the *New Masses,* announced that the autobiography would be published "next winter,"[66] and on August 6, 1934, Ornitz wrote to Communist party general secretary Earl Browder that the Stokes manuscript was "unorganized, diffuse and suffered particularly from the bourgeois tradi-tion of memoir writing," and that his poor financial circumstances and other commitments had deterred him from doing the "pains-taking and perhaps painful research." "I promise you," he said, "that my next task will be the completion of the Stokes book."[67] That promise was never fulfilled. But in what Rose Pastor Stokes was able to write she provided the vividness of recollection and emotional power that make her auto-biography a unique introduction to some of the critical events of this century.

"I Belong to the Working Class"

CHAPTER I

Childhood in Europe

I slipped into the world while my mother was on her knees, scrubbing the floor.

It was on July 18, 1879.

"Hindl the Straw Girl" they called my mother. She was so fairskinned and straight, and so slender.

She was married off at seventeen.

Her father, Berl the Fisherman, was pleased with the attention paid her by Jacob the Learned Bootmaker.

But Hindl didn't love Jacob.

She secretly adored a young Pole who was madly in love with her.

But filial piety was strong in the heart of young Hindl. She could not wound her old father. Besides, daughters did not marry—they were married off, and her father was determined upon her marriage with Jacob.

When Jacob came courting her, she smudged her face and hands, and put on a soiled gown.

But Jacob the Learned Bootmaker was not to be discouraged. Her father approved of the match. That was sanction enough for Jacob.

Berl the Fisherman made all arrangements for the wedding.

When the marriage canopy stood ready and the guests were there, and he himself came to lead his daughter to the waiting groom, he found her sitting near the tile oven in his fisherman's hut, her hair uncombed, her face unwashed, and gowned in old worn homespun.

Berl loomed before her like "the wrath of God." His powerful frame with the slightly stooped shoulders straightened like a bow freed of its string. His thinly-bearded rugged face, with its high cheek-bones, generous mouth, and kindly grey eyes gloomed darkly upon her.

"You won't go? You will go!"

For the first time in Hindl's life her father's hand came down across her cheek.

Her mother, silently weeping, helped to deck out the unweeping bride.

Her father went off for reinforcements.

When he appeared with kin and neighbors, she was literally carried to the marriage ceremony.

So Hindl the Straw Girl was married off to Jacob the Learned Bootmaker.

And they lived like strangers under a common roof. . . .

• • •

When I was nearly three years old my mother had left that common roof, and she had gone to live once more in the fisherman's hut.

Whereat Jacob the Learned Bootmaker went much farther. He left Augustova for America.

From New York City, after much pleading on the part of our kin, he granted my mother a divorce.

Yet so bound by tradition was my mother, she would not marry her Polish lover—out of the faith and against her father's will.

When I was three years old, my mother crossed the border at Koenigsburg. She went with many tears, from her old father. She was leaving her native land to seek work and life in other lands. Perhaps she was looking her last into the dear eyes, the beloved face. And I cried because my mother wept and my grandfather sobbed.

• • •

Of the first three years of my life I retain a few distinct memories:

A girl with fiery red hair rocks me in a cradle. She rocks it too hard. It turns. I fall out to the floor, and cry. . . .

"Yes" (my mother—years afterward:) "There *was* a red-haired girl, Leah, who lived in a rear room with her old mother, and helped to take care of you" . . .

Bare baby legs, mine, thrust through the palings of a balcony overlooking a square, facing a church with a tall, tall steeple.

Iron-hoofed horses, and iron uniformed soldiers of the Czar maneuver on the square. One voice, ringing steel, commands. Men and horses swing and whisk and turn and gallop, stop suddenly, race, and disappear with a *cra-kerreka! Kerreka-Kerreka!*

Then a Boom boom boom! of cannon—a new terrible sound in the world. . .

Down by a river. Sparkle . . . movement . . . flow of crystal waters. Many women bathing. My mother brings me near and nearer to the river's edge till my bare feet feel the water over them.

Sweet sunny green slope down to the slender yellow strand!

Women—bodies folded in soft white muslin, bathing, laughing, calling to each other!

A fisherman's boat on the Mazurian Lakes![1] My grandfather fishing.

I sit in a corner out of harm's way; watch him struggle with the oars, the nets, the living silver swiftness in their toils.

The world is made of water, sky, and light. In the heart of it all beams a smile—so kind! so kind! The smile of Zaidi Berl—the smile of Berl the old fisherman—my beloved grandfather . . .

My gentle little grandmother dying of the typhus. My mother casting herself upon the still form, tearing at it—"calling her back"—with a wild crying that still rings down the years. "Bringing" her "back"—to hold her again among the living for only two agonizing days more, alas!

Then the dead, laid out upon the earthen floor of the little hut,

covered with a soft old Persian shawl—a marriage gift from her mother
—and shawled women coming and going, coming and going, and mur-
muring to one another . . .

When there was still the balcony facing the public square—and my
cradle still near a tall dark cupboard, and a red-haired girl still came and
went, and my mother's face was close and dear, I remember a light little
man near a long French window looking to the square, sitting on a low
stool before a low bench, finishing a shining, shining black boot.

The movements of his arms are very swift, and light ringleted hair on
a head bent low moves with the motion of the swift arms.

The face I do not see, do not remember.

By a strange chance I am to see that face clearly once; for a few brief
moments; more than twenty years later—in America . . .

"I will take care of her," says little Samuel.

Jacob the Learned Bootmaker was a young widower with a little son
when he came to court my mother. When Jacob left for America he left
little Samuel behind. Until the day we crossed the border at Koenigsburg little Samuel lived by turns with us, and with his father's mother.
"Mother" he called my mother. He was my little playmate then. But
this is my one early memory of him!

"I will take care of her."

Samuel has me fast by the wrist. He is pulling me up the hill where a
house has burned down.

He pokes with a stick among the ruins.

He finds—oh, wonder of wonders! the porcelain head of a doll.

One side of the head is burnt black but the other side—eh! . . .

Samuel pokes again among the ruins. And now the doll's head is on
a short stick, wrapped about with a bit of charred gay colored silk . . .

That was the only doll my childhood ever knew.

Samuel? Samuel is dead now. He too went to America. For nearly
half a century he slaved early and late, living on lunches brought to the
shop. Bread and tea, a sandwich.

He made custom clothes for fine gentlemen, and died in poverty three years ago (1928), of tuberculosis in the King's County Hospital, where my old mother and I found him as he coughed the last moments of his life away . . .

I am dressed in Turkey red. A turkey gobbler is chasing me.

My mother had said turkeys chase children who wear red—and watch out for turkeys!

I hear his gobble-gobble and run to escape him . . .

Just these few simple memories of the small town in Russia where I was born, and where I lived till the age of three . . . and the town well near by grandfather's hut, and the long well-sweep. The homes of his simple neighbors. The small children who played nearby. The strain of an old lullaby sung by the baker's wife to her baby. The smell of unleavened bread freshly baked, and drawn by long-handled wooden paddles out of the deep oven. Women chattering over the rolling of fresh loaves of raw dough. An old woman plucking feathers, white feathers. The taste of honey on bread in a tiny tabernacle. My grandfather's hands as he spread the honey. A young girl holding me by the hand in a vast synagogue free of worshippers, sunlight streaming in through a tall, high window, and a bird flying in the rafters and singing . . . A large crude mangle, filled with stones, holding me, perched on top, while it rattles over great white sheets to flatten them out for the town's women-folk who washed them down by the river. The "feel" of the dirt reeds under my feet, the holes in the roads that held water after rain. The bits of flagging here and there, and the "feel" of them whenever my bare feet crossed them. . . . These and other scraps of memories I carried away with me into Germany and from thence to the city of London.

These scraps would not be worth recording, save to show the simple non-revolutionary background against which I had my beginnings.

On the wall, over the bed where my little grandmother died of the typhus, hung a large, framed, colored print—the only picture in the hut.

I remember it clearly.

It was a picture of Alexander II.

My grandfather was a simple fisherman who "made a living."

Czar Alexander II was on the wall of his fisher's hut because "The Lord" had "always put fish enough" into his nets to enable him to feed his wife and six children. The last and youngest of his children was faring forth to lands where his four sons and other daughter had gone. Now he would inhabit his fisher's hut alone. And, surely, "the Lord would provide fish" for his nets to keep him in his old age! Alexander II, Czar of all the Russias . . . even of the Mazurian Lakes . . . What a brilliant uniform! . . . What sparkling decorations! . . . A pleasant picture for the walls of a contented old fisherman's hut! . . .

• • •

On our way through Germany my mother stopped to visit her three older brothers.

All three were professional singers—cantors in their respective synagogues.

Grandfather Berl had spent the most vigorous years of his life providing musical training for his three nightingales.

Equipped for their profession, they migrated into Germany, where they readily found secure positions, married, and raised large families.

They were very respectable—living on comfortable incomes.

My memories of our three months' visit with them are a grand piano, and of a wonderful voice, singing. Another voice and another—and the strains of a violin. Long French windows, with sunlight streaming into a spacious room, falling upon a highly polished floor. Soft rugs, music—and again, rich voices singing. Soft speaking voices, silver laughter of little children. The mingled magical odors of garden and orchard, and the rich color of dahlias.

These memories were to haunt my early years in the Stony City of London.

To me, a child of three, Germany was simply a sweet place where gardens and orchards bloomed, where children laughed, and men sang; where plenty graced the table, and men murmured Grace into the ear of God, and petitioned for further plenty, while children gravely listened.

We sailed from a German port.

The seas were rough.

"Mama! Take me back to Uncle Yacob," I pleaded.

"Yes, yes, I'll take you back, by-and-by," came the gentle voice of my mother.

But she knew that she would never go back.

Her fourth brother and her only sister lived with their families in the East End of London. They were workers. She too would find work in London, and live with her simple hard-working brother and sister.

Her German brothers were too grand for Hindl who had been married off to a bootmaker—a learned man, true; but a bootmaker, nevertheless.

She was glad even of rough seas. They were bearing her far from the Three Nightingales' Germany.

Of our journey to London from whatever British port it was, I recall only a ride in the night, on a large, flat truck with iron-rimmed wheels that rattled over cobblestone roads.

On the truck were huddled between twenty and thirty immigrants, hugging their large bundles.

My mother held me close with one arm. The other was thrown across the top of a great round bundle: We were all she possessed in the world.

Through sleepy eyes I saw lights in the night; red, green, blue, yellow—so many! blinking, winking, appearing, disappearing, changing places—then no more of the journey to London Town!

• • •

A tenement room, with a bed in it, a cradle, a table, some chairs, a very small fireplace with a very little grate, and a door to another room.

My mother cooks supper on a tiny coke fire.

There is a baby in the cradle—an ailing baby.

My little Aunt Esther, herself hardly taller and no less frail than a child, goes wearily from the pot on the fire to the baby in the cradle; back to the pot on the fire, and again to the baby in the cradle.

She is anxious. She has not slept.

The baby is so white! And from time to time a thin faint wailing comes from the cradle.

Supper. We sit about the table: Four little children, my Aunt Esther and I.

Through the hall-door comes my mother.

She washes at a basin in a far corner of the room, and, weary, draws a chair to the meal.

Another—through the same door—a sister of Aunt Esther.

Her eyelids are very red. She sits silent.

Then Uncle Solomon, through the other door, enters. He takes off a short leather apron, and comes to the table.

We eat. They are all tired—too tired to talk. Only the children chatter.

The supper?

It would be one dish of something. Rice, or fish, or a stew, or pota-toes—with bread and tea.

We all sleep in those two rooms, somewhere. In the big bed—against the wall are many little arms and legs: several children, Aunt Esther and the baby, and I.

I stir in the night—become aware of breathing, warm bodies near me, of Aunt Esther stirring with the baby in her arms, and I go to sleep again—lingering in an orchard to pluck golden pears from bending boughs . . .

Early morning: I am wakened by children romping, pulling at the bedclothes. Aunt Esther is not there. The infant lies still. It is in the bed, near me. I look at the tiny face. It is so white, so still! I am awed. I do not play with the children. I sit and gaze at the still white baby. I do not know what it is that holds me, gazing, hushed. But I do not take my eyes from the little face.

My Aunt comes in; shuffles half-tense, half-tired, to the bed. She lifts the infant off the pillow, and lays it in the cradle.

She covers the child, pauses, looks to the door—expectant and waits.

Three shawled women come in. Three shawled women with solemn faces.

My Aunt hushes the romping children.

The women go to the cradle. They gaze at the baby.

One woman comes to the bed, pulls a soft white feather from the pillow, and returns to the cradle.

My Aunt stretches out a hand.

The neighbor puts the hand aside, and herself places the feather close, close against the baby's tiny nostril . . . *The feather lies still . . .*

The woman waits a few moments. Then—"It does not stir," says the woman.

Aunt Esther drops before the cradle with a strange, high wailing.

"It is dead," says one of the women.

"It is dead, Esther." And they wail with the mother of the dead.

• • •

Uncle Solomon sits in the other room, on a low stool, near a low bench that is covered with small tools and bits of leather.

He holds a shoe on a last, bending over it and pressing it deep, deep against his sunken chest. And his breath comes in short, sharp, violent explosions as he burnishes the leather, rubbing it with a small tool rapidly, and with all his strength.

He is young, very dark, very spare. His eyes are large and black and luminous—and sunken deep in their sockets. His cheeks too are sunken, and make more sharp his high cheek-bones. There is a soft, silken, black, irregular growth of beard on his face, and his mouth is soft, wide, and generous. His shoulders, frail, are slightly stooped.

He is like my grandfather—but without a boat, and the lake, and the fish.

He is like my grandfather, but sitting bent, always, always, always— over a boot burnishing it . . . And with a family to feed on a few shillings a week, says my little Aunt Esther, and grey tenements growing, looming about him—shutting him in—and the four farthings that make up the penny, shrinking—always shrinking! . . .

He hums softly, or sings in low tones: only a little and stops.

He cannot burnish his boot, and sing and hum at the same time: And the boot must be burnished, unceasingly . . .

The voice is strangely moving, even to a little child.

Uncle Solomon was the Fourth Nightingale.

But Uncle Solomon was born late.

Berl the Fisherman's head was fast turning gray when Solomon was a tall lad. He had received instruction in Talmudic lore, true—as every promising male child must, but he got no musical training.

Therefore, when young Solomon left Augustova to seek work in a strange land, he was equipped only with a few rubles and his father's tearful cry: "May you get work quickly! Solomon, my son."

When he got to London, he found work with a master bootmaker, in a small room already crowded with several apprentices.

Later, he got himself a bench at home, and took work from the new masters, the early shoe "manufacturers." Then he gave up the bench to seek work inside the factories.

Uncle Solomon seems always to be looking for work now. Mornings he starts out hopeful . . . .

Maybe . . . Maybe . . . Somewhere . . .

Evenings he returns silent, sad, his cheek-bones looking sharper, his cheeks more sunken, his eyes deeper in their sockets.

My mother works in a small tailor's shop.

Aunt Esther's sister too, works in a tailor's shop.

We live on what they get for their labor. It cannot be much.

There is little bread for long periods at a time.

The children cry, and pluck at Aunt Esther's skirts.

"Mamma, mamma, bread and treacle!"

Aunt Esther goes to the bare table, buries her head in her apron, and breaks into loud weeping.

The children hush up, and go to the street.

I remember pangs of hunger—a gnawing that would make me restless when I tried to play.

I would stop in a game of "knuckles" in the courtyard of the tenement, and look about me, bewildered. I did not know what was wrong with me, but I could not go on with the game.

When I tried to skip Dutch Rope, my legs, which had been so nimble, got tangled in the ropes.

At night, I would toss in bed, with something plucking at my vitals, and grow aware of the other children tossing too.

I would shut my eyes fast only to be teased by visions of golden pears, hanging from high branches, out of reach . . . Beyond them I would see the gentle, drawn face of my Uncle Solomon. He was hungry too . . .

There are long stretches of memory of the time before my school days began. Gray stretches.

Gray stones, gray skies, gray walls of tenements. Gray days of hunger and emptiness.

Somewhere back of Old Montague Street, in the East End of London, I played in gray courtyards.[2] There were many games, Blind Man's Buff, Puss-in-the-Corner, Hide-and-Seek, Ring-around-a-Rosie, and many more games in which we took sides, or formed circles and sang.

When I was hungry—and that was much of the time, I played without joy in the game.

There was always a group of children standing outside the nearest fried fish shop with pinched white faces and spindle legs, hushed and solemn before the teasing odor of fried plaice and fried potatoes. Or, before the baker's shop, noses pressed against the glass pane gazing and gazing at the bread-stuffs and the pastries.

Mostly, when we played we played solemnly; when we sang we sang without gladness. There was little or no laughter in our play. We played hard. We were like taut strings ready to break with a little extra pressure.

I don't remember a single scrap. But I do remember being often hurt. In games: running, leaping, jumping; striking stone walls; running blindfolded into lampposts; racing around corners; stumbling down tenement stairs; tripping over cats in the dark.

So many cats there were! Such dark stairways, and so many flights of stairs!

We were always climbing them! Up, down, up, down. Up for bread and treacle (a cheap syrup; there was never butter), down for another game; up for another slice, often to be told there was no more—down for an errand to the grocer's shop, the few farthings tightly gripped in the hand lest a precious coin slip out and be lost.

Running, racing, dashing—up, down.

Daylight or dark—it made no difference. I had no fear—had never been taught to fear, never been threatened with bogies, or ghosts, or devils. The dark was like daylight, only our eyes were different—they couldn't see in the night. We had to feel our way because our eyes were not made like cats' eyes.

Often stumbling upon one cat after another on my way up four or five flights of stairs in the deep dark, I would envy them their eyes, glowing like golden lights in the darkness.

• • •

We were living with Aunt Sarah's family when my school days began.

Aunt Sarah, my mother's only sister, was one of the elder children. She was the first to leave her father's hut.

She came to London, married, and now had a growing family. There was a girl in her teens, and boys growing into men. They were all like their mother: large; dynamic.

Uncle Solomon was working again, and did not need my mother's help now. And Aunt Sarah could spare a room for my mother and me. At Aunt Sarah's we would not be so crowded. She had a large "house." Uncle Rosenthal was making a better living.

When we came to live with her she entered me at the Chicksand Street School.

And I felt riveted to the desk. Our desks were riveted to the floor. Our teacher would command—suddenly, and suddenly we would have to take up slate and pencil or lay them down. Our eyes were nearly always on the teacher or the blackboard.

The teacher always fingered a shining, inch-square ebony ruler. She used it to strike the children so many blows across the palm of the hand, always counting them out loud as she struck, or "knuckle" them with it—much or little—depending upon how wicked we were or how angry, she.

She took kindly to me for some reason, I had never felt the sting and I enjoyed a grateful immunity from that terrible black ruler. I was an eager scholar, and learned my lessons easily. She had no reason to punish me.

But one day she punished.

We were learning the classic "Spider and the Fly." The teacher was writing two of the verses on the blackboard. I was fond of drawing. So, while the teacher wrote the verses, I busied myself with drawing on the slate. Something I drew happened to amuse me so much that laughter bubbled up in me, and spilled over.

"Come hither, hither, pretty fly!" began my teacher, and my laughter rang right out in the silent classroom.

She turned in anger.

"Rose, stop that laughter!"

I tried. For a few moments I was still.

"Come hither, hither, pretty fly," again said the teacher, and after her the class, "Come hither, hither"—

This time it was different. It bubbled up, and up, and up, and kept spilling over. I simply had to keep on laughing.

"Rose, *will you stop that laughter!*" The teacher was very angry.

"Yes, teacher," I said, sobering up, meaning it, meaning to obey "with all might!"

But, we had barely returned to the lesson when a very gale of laughter caught me.

I felt the on-coming storm from the other end of the room, but I could not stop. I laughed, and laughed, and laughed till all the children caught it, and laughed with me. Now the teacher came up the aisle. That ruler, jet black, highly polished, and an inch square, came with her.

She stepped before my desk, ruler poised.

"Rose, hold out your hand."

My hand went out—a hand that had never been struck before, not even light.

I had seen other little girls squirm and cry under the blows of that ebony stick, and my child's heart swelled in sympathy with the agonized victims. Now the little black instrument was to descend on me.

Timidly my hand went out, palm up.

The ruler descended . . . only to swish across the teacher's full dark skirts instead.

I had snatched away my hand, in time to save it the blow.

The teacher's face paled. A wild rage was behind her pallor.

"Hold–out–your–hand!" she cried.

My hand obedient went out again. And, without meaning to, it moved away again, as the shining black stick—hard as bone, sharp as knives at its four corners—came down to cut across the tender palm.

My teacher was like a Fury now.

"Hold–out–your–hand!" she shrieked.

But now, instead of doing as I was told, I placed my arms deliberately behind me, and clasped my hands against my back, as we were made to do to sit at attention.

Now nothing held the teacher. She tore my right arm forward, closed my hand, and played the dull and sharp edges of the terrible black ruler on the tender bare knuckles; beating short, hard, rapid blows upon them—long, oh long!

Yes, long enough to cripple my hand for many weeks! Long enough to have left scars that I have carried all my life where the skin had been broken; puffed, and blue, and swollen, and broken.

When her anger was spent, she returned to her desk amid the dead silence of the children. Then, perhaps, she realized what she had done.

"Take up your slates," she ordered.

Slates went out.

"Pencil in hand—ready!"

She gave dictation.

I obeyed with the rest. I stuck the slate pencil with my left hand into the swollen right that would not open. I tried to scribble—but I could not.

Now the teacher announced a recess.

I left my desk, snatched my cap and ran. I was first across the school playground, and out through the little door in the wall.

Off the school grounds, I let the tears flow, and cried all the way home.

Aunt Sarah was in the kitchen making the noon-day meal.

"What is it, woe is me! What is the matter, Rosalie, tell me!"

Between great sobs I told her what had happened, and showed her my hand.

My Aunt Sarah bristled like a thousand bayonets. She threw off her apron, and flung a huge dark shawl over her shoulders with a magnificent swing of her arm. Then she took me by the hand and said,

"Come!"

When we got to the door in the wall she swung through it, across the playground, into the building, up a few steps, down the hall a bit and into the schoolroom.

Some of the children were at their desks, and the teacher was still at hers.

Aunt Sarah stepped forward, flung back her shawl, swept up her sleeve, swung a hand across the teacher's face, swept up the other sleeve, swung the other hand across the teacher's face, took me by the hand and said, "come!" Out of the room, we strode down the hall a bit, down a few steps, out across the playground, through the little door in the wall—and home! . . .

It was hard for Aunt Sarah to move. "Even in good season we can't afford a moving day. Beside, Uncle Rosenthal is again on part-time," she said.

"Then, there's no good cause," she added. "We're not being put out by the landlord, so it's foolish to change—to go into debt for the whim of a child!"

But nothing could make me go back to the Chicksand Street School.

I was stubborn. I would even go several blocks out of my way on an errand that would have sent me past the school building.

In time, my Aunt felt sorry for the blows all around: "Poor teacher!" she mused. "Little children are starved to make a few manufacturers rich. So the world ruled by the rich is cruel to the child from the school up. Anyhow, the teacher gets three times as many children as she can with patience care for. And what do they pay her? And I have to go and quarrel with the teacher, who is herself a worker; and who can't help the way things are. Go back, Rosalie, maybe she'll be better now."

"No, I won't go back, I won't!" And I became a truant.

• • •

In that long, long period of truancy I discovered a new and thrilling game.

Was it in the Whitechapel Road? . . . It was on a wide thoroughfare where omnibuses ran. At a point where people changed 'buses. At any rate a point where they threw away their fare slips, pink, blue, red, yellow. . . .

On the back of these slips little verses were printed, of four lines each and of infinite variety.

In the clanging, rushing traffic I would risk my life daily to gather up the precious slips that lay right out in the middle of the road.

Dodging under 'buses and carts and hansom cabs I would rescue as many as my two hands could hold, run off to a stone stoop, or to church steps, or to a slab in the churchyard, and feast my soul on "poetry."

Every verse ended with the word SAPOLIO! in great big letters, and with a grand flourish. I did not know who or what was sapolio. But I discovered that words arranged in singing measure, words that rhymed and had rhythm, were an unending delight.

During that long period out of school, I wandered about the district as I pleased. Sights and sounds and smells of the East End—mostly grey sights, harsh sounds, smells not so good; forgotten now, save the bad smell of musty houses and cellars, and the good smells of fried plaice and fried potatoes.

Once on a Saturday afternoon, I stray far from home, follow a stream of folk who drift through a little doorway in a stone wall—and suddenly, I find myself in a courtyard, in an undreamed of sunny, quiet place. Green ivy covers the walls on every side, and doves—living, moving, cooing doves with bright wings move about the sunny place and make a strange sweet sound with their quivering throats! . . . I stand still. And the birds move close, closer! They do not fly away! They come *right up to my feet*! All the while making that strange, moving sound with their throats . . . I am ready to cry out with ecstasy.

But the stream of folk still move on . . . I follow. Through another arched doorway . . . a little doorway across the courtyard . . . up a stairway . . . into a large room. The walls are hung with pictures . . . I wander about and marvel until I come to one—and stop. I do not move for a long, long time, but stand and gaze. It is the picture of a woman . . . the nude body of a woman. Beautiful! more beautiful than anything I have ever seen before . . . I drift out with the crowds. I drift homeward. All the way I am filled with a strange "high" feeling . . . I must come back to this place . . . I think. And soon I start on my adventure. But I cannot find the way. I search and search—going up and down that wide thoroughfare and into side streets, but never find that little doorway again. . . .

Such wanderings, however, are not a part of my "schooling."

"She'll have to go to school somewhere," said my Aunt Sarah, and moved close to Frying Pan Alley in the neighborhood of the Jewish Free School.

Here she registered me. "Name?" asked a woman at a desk.

"Rose Rosenthal," said my Aunt, with a gesture of proprietorship.

So "Rose Rosenthal" in school I was.

My teacher's name happened to be so nearly like mine—Ray Rosenthal—that everything in class (First Standard) looked right and happy again.

Here I was taught little songs and poems, and trod on clouds between home and school.

I never owned a book. A book was a fairy tale that never comes true. And it was out of a book (in the First Standard) that my teacher taught us poems and songs. I learned these "by heart" as naturally and easily as a bird sings—and I moved in a new air.

◆ ◆ ◆

When I was in my ninth year, my mother thought she would marry again. She had had a number of offers, but there was one—well—!

However, being Berl the Fisherman's daughter still, she decided to write her old father about it, and ask his advice.

Berl the Fisherman had been having many good hauls, and with none but himself to care for, had laid by enough money to pay a visit to London. So he came to see for himself whether the man who wanted his daughter for wife was a good and worthy man.

Grandfather Berl stayed long enough to discover that the man smoked on the Sabbath, and forbade the match.

My mother cried in the night, when only I heard her.

By day she pleaded with her father—but he was unbending.

"What! a Goy you will marry, and let me go back to die in grief and shame!"

My mother yielded.

She broke off her engagement to the kind, devoted "Goy," and returned the ring he had given her.

Grandfather Berl went back to his fisher's hut to end his declining days in peace and content.

◆ ◆ ◆

Much "company" came to our tenement rooms.

They stayed late in the evenings, and talked of many things. Religion—my grandfather's kind; the new kind, wages, the workers; the shops; the masters.

I would sit in a deep corner of the room, unnoticed, and listen. I never tired of hearing the talk. I would have understood little of it all. But something must have sunk in.

I remember going about with a new notion in my head.

There is no Heaven elsewhere . . . Earth will be Heaven someday . . . We'll live in peace with one another . . . We'll learn to live on and on and on! . . . There will be no dying . . . We'll learn how to live on without end—here, here on earth. . . .

My mother was the life of these gatherings. She argued, opposed, attacked, defended. She would have learned when in those discussions— got ideas she had never had before.

Mainly they talked of the shops.

"In my shop, the master never pays a farthing for overtime."

"In our shop, the master drives us to death. We haven't swallowed our tea before he shouts 'Back to the machines!'"

"Where I work, the W.C. (excuse me!) is so filthy that we'd rather get sick than use it."

"Sixteen shillings and sixpence! And we worked like horses! Are we cattle to be driven like that? or dogs to be given a bone?"

". . . sent them home because they came a few minutes late. Think of it, a few minutes late! . . ."

"If they'd stand together, they'd show the masters! . . ."

When they wearied of talk someone would start singing; usually, my mother. Her voice was clear and sweet, and every word of the song was heard. Her singing was so heartsome, that soon all would be joining in, while she and my Aunt Esther—with whom we were again boarding— would serve tea in tall glasses.

The songs they sang were of labor, and of a popular operetta called "Shulamith."

One day I came home from school at the noon hour to find my mother at home, pacing the floor and talking excitedly to Aunt Esther.

I glowed with the unexpected pleasure of seeing her and rushed to embrace her.

She kissed me as if I wasn't there, and kept on talking and pacing up and down.

My aunt stood before the fire drinking in every word. And my mother's words sank deep into me too.

"So a few of us girls who sat near the windows would sometimes lift our eyes from the work, and look out on the street.

"Well? A human being is not a horse, or a cow. And even cows and horses want to poke a nose out of a stall sometimes, to see the world outside.

"But no! not a worker! The master would like to take our eyes out, but he needs them; they are useful to him—they watch the sewing. Girls' eyes were made to glue on a seam; ten hours a day, twelve hours a day! Follow the seam! Follow the seam! Not a moment to lose! Not a moment!

"There's a living, moving world outside—full of light, full of color! There's life, life out there, but not for you—not even to look at through dusty window panes!

"The world is for me and mine! says the master.

"So what did he do—our master? What do you think he did?

"He whitewashed those windows. Yes, whitewashed them."

"Whitewashed!" My Aunt Esther's timid little voice came high and thin after my mother's voice, rich and vibrant.

"Yes, whitewashed! We came this morning to find them whitewashed!

"Are we slaves? Are we prisoners? Are we already among the dead that these shards are laid upon our eyes?" My mother flung out her arms as if she were talking to a multitude.

"I turned right to the workers: Will you stand for it? Will you allow him to lay us, living, in a tomb? For the sake of a few measly farthings? Will you? I'd starve first!

"The master was downstairs. I took my apron, folded it, and said: 'Come, girls, come down. We'll strike!' And, *Estherke*, my life, they folded their aprons and came down with me.

"We have a picket-line—formed right on the spot! And the master—he's in a fit!

"'Don't you dare to come back to my shop,' he said to me, purple in the face, 'or I'll pitch you through the window! I will!'

"'Oh, I'll come back!' I told him, 'I'll come back! Mr. Blank, but those windows will be clean—and you'll put your lovely whitewash on those dingy walls instead!'"

For a week my mother came and went, with flashes of anger, defiance, humor; reporting progress, and rushing away to the battle-line.

A week and the strike was over. The workers had won!

The master wanted to keep my mother out. But the others refused to return without her.

She came back in triumph. The windows were clear, and the dingy walls of the workshop were whitewashed!!

Thereafter, my mother never failed to agitate other workers, and exhort them to have courage and defy the masters; and she would always tell the story of her strike.

And a striking worker is forever afterward different from one who has never been on the picket-line.

• • •

One Sunday my mother gave me an extra good scrubbing and hurried me into a clean frock.

"There's going to be a party," was all she said, "so keep clean Rosalie."

Later, my Aunt Esther took me aside and explained:

"Your mother is getting engaged today. The party will be this afternoon. Keep your dress clean, and your hands and face. And when he come, you must give him a kiss—yes?"

Another "desecrater of the Sabbath"! My mother was going to marry him, and my orthodox grandfather could no longer interfere: Berl the Fisherman had died that year.

After my mother's engagement to the tall broad-shouldered young Rumanian from Yassy, with the reddish-brown hair and brown eyes, the bristling mustaches, and the deeply arched brows, there were many evenings of song, story and tea-drinking.

Sometimes it was beer as well as tea. And I—downstairs and up—upstairs and down to the Public House for a draft of ale, for a quart of "arf-and-arf" and back.

And then, at last, out of breath but happy to become part of the company, I would sit in a corner unnoticed and listen to the talk and the singing.

One evening there was great excitement. The young Rumanian had received a letter from home informing him of the death of an uncle. The uncle had left some money, and he must return at once to claim his share.

A fortune! What luck! Gatherings of family, friends. And what consultations!

The wedding was set off. The Rumanian sailed to claim his fortune.

Letters came from Yassy almost daily. These my mother would read, part to herself, part aloud to the family, and her face would glow with happiness.

About a week before the wedding the prospective groom returned. And now there was money! My mother went on shopping tours with her Rumanian, while I would post myself on a balcony of the tenement and gaze down the street, refusing to eat my supper—watching, watching for the beloved form, never certain till I caught sight of her far down the street, coming near and nearer, that she would ever again return to me—that she would not be spirited away by that young lover of hers who took so much of her time from me. When she delayed till dark I was in tears, and ineffably happy when she appeared—just as I thought I had lost her forever!

After my mother's marriage to Israel Pastor, the young Rumanian, we three lived in a diminutive court somewhere in the neighborhood of Frying Pan Alley.

Two rows of tiny houses faced each other across the narrowest space imaginable. Five or six of these houses were on either row. Every little street door led to a tiny room which had a tiny fireplace. A tiny winding stair led to a tiny upstairs room.

One of these diminutive two-room houses became our home for a while. We had barely moved in when "Jack the Ripper,"[3] the terror of London, deposited the torso of one of his victims under a barrow close to our court. But my mother did not share the terror that possessed the folk about us. And I too was not afraid, passing at night the barrow and the very spot where the "horror" was discovered without feeling fear.

My step-father bought me a dress of Scotch plaid, a tam o'shanter hat of black velvet and a pair of red silk stockings and black patent leather shoes; and sometimes he would take me to one of the theatres on the Whitechapel Road, and on the way buy me my favorite chocolate buttons.

He loved my mother, and was very kind to me.

"Call him father," my mother said. And I called him father, even through the years.

During the time we lived in the tiny court, Israel Pastor had put his "fortune" into plate glass and a partner. It was not long before he lost a good bit of the "fortune" and his partner turned out to be a "scoundrel" with whom he was compelled to break.

He had worked in a cap factory once. His master had made plenty of money. . . . Why not a cap factory?

We move to Black Lion's Yard, off the Whitechapel Road.

Our living quarters are on the ground floor.

Upstairs are large workrooms: sewing machines, workmen, tables, presses, cutters, steam, talk, song and clatter.

Often after school I go up to the workroom and stand silent near a driven machine. I watch the man who drives it. I wish that he would stop. "Stop, Mister, Stop!"

Most of the time I am downstairs with my mother.

In the evenings there would be talk between my mother and father.

They would sit before the little coal-grate and worry about the men upstairs.

"Abraham the operator spits blood. I saw it."

"Yes, he's got the consumption."

"I can't bear to watch him driving that machine, day after day."

I ask what is the consumption. My mother tells me.

"It breaks the heart, child!" Tears fill my mother's eyes. My father draws her head to his shoulder and his own eyes are moist.

Abraham was so ill, he had to be brought down to the couch in the front room.

We all took care of him. My father paid for doctor and medicine, and sent money home to his wife and child.

Abraham the operator died, and was buried from the house in Black Lion's Yard. And Israel Pastor, my stepfather, continued to send money home to the wife and child of the dead worker.

Something seemed to be the matter with every worker: sickness; misery; confinements; ailing old folks; an ailing child; a funeral—always something.

My parents were unable to separate themselves from the workers. In fact, they never tried.

Israel Pastor, cap "manufacturer," did not last long. His business went rapidly downhill, and he had to give up the factory.

When everything was sold, or given for goods bought, he was left with little enough, and not unhappy to be out of it.

"Well," said he, "poor workers we'll remain."

"Better so," said my mother.

"Are all workers poor?" I ask.

"All workers," my mother replies.

"And the masters?"

"They lord it over the workers," said my mother. "It is their world."

"Father, don't be a master again," I plead.

"No, Rosalie, I won't. By-and-bye, I'll go to South America. There I will make a living, somehow; and send for you and mother and—and—the baby."

And so, simply, I was told that a baby was coming, and that father, who won't try to be a master anymore, was going to a far country to see if he can make a living some way—without "lording it" over anybody.

◆ ◆ ◆

I am in a little sweets shop on Whitechapel near the corner of Black Lion's Yard.

I had left my mother sitting by the tiny grate fire with the new baby in her lap, in the cheerful glow of coals, red-and-gold wallpaper and gaslight, to get my favorite chocolate buttons for the penny my father had given me.

I am waiting my turn. Waiting for the round-faced woman behind the counter to say in her cheery voice, "Well, little girl, and what will *you* have?"

The door opens, and a cold blast blows a beggar into the shop.

He goes to the counter and asks for something.

I don't hear what. I am more eyes and heart than ears.

He wears no hat, and the light snowfall has left cold crystals in his snow-white drift of hair.

His coat is ragged, his breast bared, his sleeves short, his wrists and hands blue with the cold. *And his feet are naked.* Large feet—naked, and blue, and swollen . . .

He has asked for something and been denied.

He turns, looks at me, looks about him, turns again and drifts out.

Three young fellows standing in the rear of the shop, laugh . . .

The woman turns to me sweetly.

"And what will *you* have, little girl?"

"I? I? . . . Nothing."

I turn from the counter and look about me, not knowing what to do. I am vaguely aware of the woman, of the boys, of their laughter.

I grip the penny tightly in my hand, and stand still without thinking things—just stand there; then fly to the door in panic, and rush out.

I look up the street. Where is he—where?

Through the snow flurry in the dusk, I think I see a white-haired man far down the street. I run fast. I am out of breath . . . It is not he. Could he have gone the other way? I run down Whitechapel. I pass many people. I peer through shop windows. Maybe . . . ! No, I cannot find him!

Where is he—the homeless man with the snow-white hair, with the frozen hands, with the naked feet pressing the snow, treading the bitter pavements? Where is he who asked for something—bread, or a crust, or a farthing—and was denied?—and laughed at?

The tears are streaming down my face. I am running home with my grief—when, down the narrow sidewalk, near the street lamp at the other end of the court, I see—a figure! My heart leaps. With pity; with joy! It is he! I have found him! found him! . . .

I run fast. I am breathless when I catch up with him. I touch his arm tightly, tightly. I look up into his face. My eyes are so blurred I scarcely see . . . "Will you take my penny, please?" He takes it, and puts a large, frozen, blue hand on my head, and says brokenly, "God bless you, little girl!"

And I sob aloud with heartbreak, as I stand and watch him drift past the lamppost and disappear around the corner.

I return to the warm room with the red-and-gold wallpaper and the glowing hearth. My mother is still sitting near the fire, and the baby on her knee. She is alarmed at my tears.

"What is the matter? Rosalie, what it is?"

I cannot speak.

"Did you lose your penny?"

I shake my head, and continue to sob.

"Then where are your chocolate buttons?"

I cannot answer. I can only weep.

"But what is the matter? What has happened?"

My father comes in.

"What is it? Rosalie, did someone steal your penny? Here, I'll give you another one."

Between sobs, brokenly, I tell them.

My mother kisses me.

"Yes, yes, child mine, we know! Don't cry, don't cry so!"

My father strokes my curls.

"Don't cry, Rosalie, don't cry. I'll give you another. Look, a bran' new penny!"

But I am uncomforted.

How could I tell them it was not a new penny, but a new world I wanted, when I myself was not aware? . . .

• • •

My father gave my mother a few gold sovereigns, bought himself a steamship ticket with what remained of his "fortune," and sailed for Buenos Aires. He had heard that in South America anyone willing to work can make a living.

"It will not be long before I'll send for you," he said, as he bade us an affectionate good-bye.

• • •

We are living in one small room in Red Lion Court. ("Puma Court" when re-visited in the spring of 1914.)

My mother takes in a lodger, an elderly woman, to share the room rent. The elderly woman takes in work. We do the same. I run to a shoe factory to fetch the raw material, then back to return the finished product. The elderly woman, my mother and I sit at a table in our room and make black satin bows for ladies' slippers. I've stopped going to school (in the middle of the Second Standard). I work all day. I rock the baby brother with my foot, and my hands fly. The needle goes in and out, in and out—and the little black satin bows are such dainty things! . . . Still, we don't get enough to keep the room and have the food we need. Sometimes, my mother speaks anxiously of truant-officers; but, somehow, I escape.

I find more work to do: I have stood in line with many other children, and was taken on.

Nights now I am on the stage of the Princess Theatre, Whitechapel. I wear several changes of fine clothing—silks and velvets, and smooth satins. I have a few speaking lines. It is a sort of pageant play, and instructs all poor little boys that they may become Lords Mayor of London, some day—just like Dick Whittington who started from home with nothing but his cat! . . .

A Mr. Cohen pays off on Saturday nights. I hurry home with a couple of crowns and several shillings tightly gripped in my little fist. On the way, I think; "If—if anyone should try to take these from me before I bring them to my mother, I—I'll fight! I'll scratch and scream, and I won't let go! Maybe they'll ask me 'Oxford or Cambridge?' and I don't know what to say, and they'll take my money! . . . I'll fight—oh, I'll fight! . . ."

♦ ♦ ♦

There was no time to play any more; save early Saturday mornings. Before anybody was awake, I'd leap out of bed, slip on frock and shoes without stopping to button them, and rush down to the court the moment I caught the first notes of the hurdy-gurdy man. He would always open with an Irish jig, and "Reddy" and I who had more dance in our feet than any of the other children in the Court would fly about in joyous rhythm with the rapid music of the street organ.

Then there was my treasure—reserved for half-hours stolen from sleep—the only book I had ever owned; the only book I had ever read: Lamb's *Tales from Shakespeare*. It was really not meant for me, but I had earned it by sympathy. It was given to Annie Berman, winner of "First Prize for Scholarship" in the Second Standard during my last school days. Annie Berman had tears in her eyes when she saw the splendor of the covers of the Second Prize—mine. "Rose, will you change with Annie?" asked my teacher, and feeling sorry for Annie's tears, I offered my book for hers. So, my school days over, I sat for magical moments before noble drama, instead of dipping as I might have done, into the tales of dwarfs and hobgoblins that lay between the covers of splendor that so attracted Annie!

Often, returning late at night from the Princess Theatre, I'd take up my book for a few moments of high delight. Lost in wonder at the tangled lives of lords and ladies, of kings and queens, I would forget, for a space, our poverty and our struggles.

At odd times, I go to Spitalfields, just outside of the court. The "Salvation Army" stations itself in a little knot near the market place. They sing. I do not know what salvation means, nor what is an army. But I love song. I stop and catch every note, every word . . .

> Rescue the perishing, care for the dying,
> Jesus is merciful, Jesus will save!

I do not know who Jesus is; do not care, do not ask.

At the table I sit and make black satin bows for ladies' slippers at a few pennies a gross. We hunger, we perish for rest, for a little joy, and I sing—*Rescue the perishing, care for the dying*—

I think of the infant who died. I think of my Uncle Solomon who works so hard, and looks so hungry and so sad; of the man with the white hair, and the frozen feet bare to the icy paving stones; I think of the woman I saw in the shadow of the big church at Church Street around the corner; of those in dark doorways and alleyways, or sprawled along the deep churchyard wall at night, revealing hideous running sores; distorted diseased arms, legs, chests, thighs; noses half-eaten away; eyes and faces bleary and brutal with drink; dirt and vermin on their bodies and on their evil-smelling rags . . . they are paralytic, sticking pins into their arms and feeling nothing! The vicious and depraved whom little children instinctively avoid . . . The poor, the submerged, the sick, the outcast, the agonized . . .

Rescue the perishing, care for the dying . . .

I think of the lords and ladies in the land. I have seen their fine mansions from the tops of omnibuses. I have looked with the awe of a child of Poverty upon the shining brass knockers on their doors. I have seen Victoria, on her Diamond Jubilee, ride by in her carriage; a plain, heavy, beak-nosed old woman of whom I have been taught, in school, to sing "God save our gracious Queen! Long live our noble Queen!" and she was attended by thousands of dressed-up lackeys! . . .

"The rich live on the poor. The masters lord it over the workers," says my mother . . .

Rescue the perishing, care for . . .

"Say!" I ask my red-headed dancing partner, "who's Jesus?"

"Oh, don't you know? For instance, tomorrow is Christmas. Tonight you pray to Jesus to send you something, and when you wake in the morning, you find it under your pillow."

"Is it really so?" (How hungry I was for an orange!)

"Yes, it's so. You'll see!"

I go to bed that night, thinking in my heart, "Jesus, please send me an orange!"

In the morning I look under the pillow—and—there is nothing!

"Well?" asked Red Head that day, "did you get something?"

"No, nothing at all."

"Oh!" her face fell.

One day, as we sat at work, the sounds of a brass band came up the court from Spitalfields.

My mother, babe in arms, shoved aside the satin bows, took mine out of my hand, motioned to the elderly woman, and said "Come!" We were hustled out of the room, down the one short flight of stairs, to the end of Red Lion Court, and out to Spitalfields.

Columns of workmen were marching down the street. As they streamed past a big, shuttered shoe factory their band struck up a funeral march.

My mother laughed and clapped her hands and called "*bravo!*"

"What's it all about?" a little knot of neighbors asked. My mother explained with great zest, as they stood near her, watching the ranks file by.

"Shoe workers on strike. They won't take a cut in wages. Can't live on what they're getting *now!* And still the masters want to cut! Not making enough profit, they're not! . . . A funeral march—that's the thing to play for 'em! Keep those shutters up, till ye win! Show the masters! Show 'em what we can do when we stick together! . . ."

She waved an arm to the ranks as they came by. Some of the men waved to her, and called defiance to the masters, and laughed gaily.

My mother's words to the neighbors told me the story of the endless line of marching men, and the mocking music for the shut-down factory—my first contact with the organized struggle, and to be always vividly remembered.

On May Day my mother took me to Hyde Park. Perhaps she was too busy looking and listening to interpret the day to me or, maybe she herself knew little of its meaning. There were crowds wherever we moved. Men talked from the ends of cart-tails. Knots of men and women collected and listened. We moved from place to place. I never saw so many people before. My mother was restless, and dragged me about until I was tired. But she did not tell me things—did not try to make me see what she herself was trying to see—to learn.

So the thing that impressed me most that day was not May Day and its meaning, but the fact that, when changing 'buses on the way home a drunken conductor gave us transfers without collecting our fares.

My mother was glad!

"The Company has plenty of the worker's money!" said my mother.

◆ ◆ ◆

When the baby was six months old, my father returned from Buenos Aires.

In one of those periodic political revolutions in the Argentine, the little money he had worked for—starving himself to save enough to settle there—had so depreciated in value that he decided to return to London. But in London times were hard. And far-away lands were a lure to both my father and my mother. Israel Pastor again booked passage. This time, for North America.

In North America there was plenty of work to be had. The American Agencies were crying for workers. "Plenty to do! Only come! From all lands—come!"

"So I'll try my luck there, and send for you as fast as ever I can," said my father.

How happy my mother was to see him again!

She spoke words of hope and courage to him before he sailed away.

"Maybe—yes, maybe. The world can't be so bad everywhere for workers, as it is here! . . ."

My step-father settled in Cleveland. Four months later, we received money for steamship tickets. My mother, my baby brother, and I started out for the new world in the autumn of 1890. I was eleven. I had had one year and a half at school, and a year of wage labor. During my eight years in London I did not remember seeing a tree or a blade of grass near my home save in a graveyard, and in the lost courtyard. There were grass and trees elsewhere in London. Once I was close enough to touch them—in a park—Victoria Park—far from my home. A few times, from the tops of 'buses, passing where the rich had their mansions, I saw green leaves and gay flowers. A few times, near the Tower of London, I saw black ravens on green grass. During those eight years there was never enough to eat. Now we were going to a far country where I hoped there would be grass and trees to enjoy—and bread—enough bread to eat.

I said goodbye to Mr. Cohen. "Hah! this *h'is* a bloomin' shime!" he said. "Cawn't ye stay 'ere? We'll mike a grite little h'actress of ye, if ye don." I thanked him, but had visions of the process: Would he jerk me about and slap my face—as he did that tall, blonde girl in the rehearsals? . . .

CHAPTER II

Coming to America

The ship we sailed in was an unseaworthy tub.

The passengers were anxious. My mother mingled much with them.

She was always explaining to her fellow voyagers: "Our lives are risked to pile up riches for the company."

We had hardly got out to sea when a storm tore a great hole in the old vessel.

Deep down in the ship men and women walked in water to their knees. Men in blue coats and gold buttons came down to quiet the panic. But when the water rose still higher—when tables, benches, boxes, and trunks began to swirl about, a great wailing went up.

In the midst of it all, a woman in black knelt up to her armpits in the water, holding high above her head a black crucifix, and crying over and over again, "Bozshe moi! Bozshe moi! Bozshe moi!"

My mother sat quietly on a box with her baby, while we watched the crazed woman. I sat beside my mother, with a hand on her arm. I was not afraid. Perhaps because my mother showed no sign of excitement. Perhaps because no one had ever taught me to be afraid.

An officer called down: "Stop your crying! We'll soon be safe in a port." Some would not believe it. But we really docked at Antwerp. For two days we were boarded in houses near the docks. When the ship was patched up, we were herded down into the bowels of her again, and once more set out on a rough voyage. Storms tossed us about. Sickness beset us down in steerage. Bodies were wrapped in canvas and buried at sea. Potatoes and herring, with bread and great chunks of salt butter (or what looked like butter) was the only food we were given. Men and women protested. They formed in groups and demanded a change, but none was made.

At the end of three weeks we steamed into New York harbor. It was early dawn. Every window on shore threw back at us bursts of golden sunlight; but the cold air, with steel fingers, gripped body.

With both hands I clutched a thin little jacket close to my shivering frame, and stared at the flaming windows; thinking: "Somewhere in this city is Jacob the Learned Bootmaker."

Now there was confused running, hither and yon. My mother took me by the hand.

"Come, Rosalie," she said, "we'll soon be in Castle Garden."[1]

Immigrants leaning against huge round bundles, exhausted with waiting, crying infants, restless children, men and women calling to each other across wide spaces. Iron pillars, iron gratings, stone walls—floors —all so cold and forbidding . . . A gnawing hunger . . . Children crying, "Bread, Mama!" Mothers slapping their children, pushing them away. "What can I give you?—I've got nothing!" "Is it my fault? wait! Wait till we get out of here—wait!"

Waiting—still waiting. Complaints, protests. Men in uniform shoving bundles about; reading labels; pushing from them complaining men, women; hurling oaths at them; calling shameful names . . . "Wait, can't you? you—! We've waited longer for you! Waddeye think America is, anyway—a banquet hall? Keep-your-shirt-on! . . ." And I thinking, "How and why is it a garden? And how long must we stay in this garden?" The time seemed endless. When a large group of us were herded on a ferry boat for New Jersey, I was so weak from hunger that my legs refused to carry me. A man in a blue coat with gold buttons grudgingly lifted me in his arms and carried me to the boat. Here my mother counted out a number of coins. A peddler took them, and gave me my first taste of bananas.

My mother lacked the money to pay our fares to Cleveland, so an official gave us an address and put us on a train. At Philadelphia, in a boarding-house for immigrants, we waited for nearly a week before my stepfather sent us the money. He had a struggle raising it, and most of it was borrowed.

• • •

On the upper floor of a two-story frame structure in the rear of Number Four Liberal Street, my stepfather ushered us proudly and happily into a three-room flat.

There was a kitchen stove (invitingly warm!). There were tables, and beds, and chairs, and a clock; oilcloth on the kitchen table, and a gaily patterned linoleum on the kitchen floor.

My mother went from one room to another, her face shining.

My stepfather came after her, the baby on his arm, a happy light in his eyes.

"Oh, Israel!" my mother turned her glowing face to him. "You bought all this!"

"All this," he said, waving an arm at the new things.

"You must be earning good money."

"Not so bad," he remarked.

Something in his tone brought another question.

"Israel—is it all—paid for?"

"Well—" And seeing the shadows creep into my mother's eyes, he put an arm about her and kissed her.

"Never mind, Hindl, don't worry. I'll pay—in good time."

That evening, after I had rocked the baby to sleep and crept into my new cot, I heard two troubled voices talking from the kitchen. They were discussing me. What to do with me. Earnings were low, times were hard, and getting worse from day to day. Everywhere it was the same. All the neighbors were in debt. The grocer, the baker, the butcher, were beginning to shut down on credit. The Feinbergs downstairs were sending their daughter to get work in a cigar factory. Maybe I'd get work if I went along. If I got work where Jennie did, she could wait for me mornings and evenings, till I learned to find the way by myself . . .

Two days later Jennie, a tall dark raw-boned girl of thirteen, started out for the job in the cigar factory, and I went with her.

As we were leaving Jennie's kitchen in the cold and the dark, my mother kissed me, and my stepfather patted my head and gave me a dime.

They both laughed with forced gaiety:

"Look! Our little breadwinner," my mother chuckled, through tears.

And my stepfather too, with a catch in his voice: "Our Rosalie, already a working woman!"

◆ ◆ ◆

We start out at dawn to be there before others fill the places.

The air is sharp with early frost. My thin jacket is like a sieve against the wind. I hold it tightly—with both hands to my chest and throat—as if the clutch of my hands could protect me.

Jennie too must be cold. She shivers.

"Come on, we must hurry!" She grips me by the hand. She is taller than I, and takes longer strides. Every few steps, I run to keep up with her.

The long way seems endless. Down the muddy unpaved street at right angles to Liberal Street. A turn to the right, then to the left down Orange Street. Down Broadway, on to the end of Ontario Street. Across the Public Square, dodging a confusing network of streetcars. Then left, for several blocks to the viaduct, and down—steeply, to a street under it. We've walked miles and miles, it seems.

Near the end of this street Jennie finds the number she has on a slip of paper. We enter the big loft building, our hearts pounding. We hold hands and climb two flights of stairs.

There are two doors: Maybe it's this one. Timidly, we push open a heavy metal door. The suffocating effluvium of tobacco dust strikes us in the face.

I want to run away from the unexpected offense. But I stand still beside Jennie, and continue to hold her hand.

There are many workers here—at work—benches all of new wood. A row each, facing the two long walls of the narrow left; in the middle, two rows facing each other built as of one piece. The bodies of the workers move in short sharp rhythm as the hands roll dark brown sticks on a board, or cut dark brown leaves into patterned pieces, or chop the ends off the sticks with a small cutting-tool.

A man comes out of a newly-partitioned office near the door. A very comfortable-looking man. I have never before been talked-to by anyone so comfortable-looking—not even Mr. Cohen of the Princess Theatre.

"I'm Mr. Wertheim," he says. "Do you want work?"

"Yes, please."

Turning to Jennie: "How old are you?"

"Fourteen," and Jennie gets very red in the face.

"A fine big girl for fourteen," Mr. Wertheim says, placing a hand on her broad, square shoulders.

"And you?"

"Eleven."

"You're tall for your age, but—" he trails off.

Does he mean not to give me work? My heart beats! And something pounds in my throat and tightens it.

"What do you say to going right to work?"

He is including us both in his look! The blood that was pounding through my heart and clutching at my throat goes to my head.

We nod our yes, and at the same moment I think of the two troubled voices from the kitchen, and go dizzy with joy in the thought of being able to help.

"Oh, Jake, two more new ones," he calls to a large heavy-featured man.

The man leaves a bench where he is teaching a young worker, and comes to the door.

"The foreman," Mr. Wertheim explains. "He'll teach you stogie-rolling."

As we go with the foreman, Mr. Wertheim offers tersely:

"Two weeks to learn. After that half-pay for six weeks, then full pay. All right?"

Had he announced six months without pay we would have nodded our heads just the same.

At the end of the third week I get three silver quarters and two copper pennies—my first week's pay.

I run home with the treasure.

My mother takes it from me, looks long at the coins in the open palm of her hand, and with a bitter cry throws them on the table.

"The blood of a child! Look," she says, "look what it will bring!"

On a Friday morning, Mr. Wertheim came and stood behind my chair.

"Rose Pastor, how would you like to go home today, and help your mother? I'll bet she needs you. I'm sure she works very hard. You can come back Monday morning, and it will be all right."

Who would have thought a boss could be so kind! I thanked him and hurried home, glad to be of help to my mother.

She always had a burden of work to do, especially on Fridays. I scrubbed the kitchen floor, and ran errands to the grocer's, and filled the oil lamps, and brought up coal, and washed the baby's things down by the yard pump; and all the time I did my chores, I overflowed with gratitude toward the boss who spoke so feelingly of my poor overburdened mother.

On Monday morning, when I came to my work-bench, I said to the girl on my right—

"Wasn't Mr. Wertheim kind?"

"Kind?" The girl on my right chuckled, "It's a good thing you were sent home Friday morning. The factory inspector came in the afternoon. Some of the young ones can sit on two extra blocks, and look over fourteen. But not you."

Jennie too never told me till Monday:

"Oh, I passed. I look old. Mr. Wertheim didn't want to lose you, I guess, so he sent you home."

"Lose me?" I asked.

"Yeah!" said the girl on my right, "Lose ye, is what she said. The younger and quicker ye are, the more money the boss makes on ye— see?"

That evening, sitting at the kitchen table, eating supper, I regarded my kind stepfather. He was only a poor peddler. True he had a horse and wagon of his own, but he wasn't a boss: I could love and respect him.

My mother got acquainted with the neighbors, and they came in— evenings, or Sunday afternoons. There was much talk, and my child's horizon again began to widen through the equal sorrows and bitter economic struggles of the little proletarian world about me. It was a hard winter. There was always someone losing a job, or hopelessly in search of one. Or the school children were without shoes or decent clothing. Or there was nothing to pay the grocer who refused further credit. Or someone came to borrow an egg for a sick child. Or the eternal Installment Plan Agent had been and threatened to take away everything unless something was paid on account—and with more than half already paid out! Or there was nothing toward the rent, most of the next month gone, and the landlord knocking daily at the door. Or there was an eviction threatened, and not a dollar to move with. Or a baby about to be born, and where will they get ten dollars for the midwife? Or someone suddenly taken ill, and which doctor will come and then wait for his money? Or a worker short-waged at the end of the week; exchange of experience with "docking" and other abuses in the shops. Or the bitter cold, and the problem of bed covers . . . No one had enough . . . Or coal; its price by the ton, and the big difference in cost to the poor who must buy by the sack. Or the advantage of one job over another. Or the disadvantage of working far from home; the cost in carfares; the loss in time; in sleep; in pay, through starting the day too tired. Or, we'd visit the neighbors; come, perhaps, when there was a quarrel—always over an economy; questions of nickels and dimes; of what to buy and what to save; of what should or should not have been done when there's so little money and one never sure of one's job.

Our lives were like our neighbors' lives. The Installment man came Monday mornings. There was not always the dollar to give him. We would take the money from the bread we needed, to pay for the blankets we needed as much. The same blankets, in the store, were half the price. All the neighbors knew it. My mother discovered it for herself. She raged against the Installment Robbers. "But how many poor workers are there who can buy for cash? Yes! That's why these leeches can drain our blood on the Installment Plan!"

"Father, don't buy any more on the Plan," I urged. "It's terrible. Mother cries when you're not here to see. We can go without things."

"Go without? No, daughter, we can't go without beds, and covers, and a stove, and tables, and chairs! And we get these things the best way we can. We can't just lie down and die!"

"We could buy *old* things, maybe," I said.

"The second-hand stuff you can pick up around here isn't fit to live with. Do you think I'd get such things—for Mother?"

He loved my mother. He would have given her the moon and stars for playthings had he been able. The least he could bear to let her have were the few cheap new things he was paying on. His work kept him driving his horse and wagon about the city—often, in the avenues of the wealthy. Sometimes he'd be called into the homes of the rich to cart away old magazines, or bottles, or rags, or old plumbing material, or discarded what-not. He knew the beautiful things the rich lived with. He saw the insides of their homes with his own eyes. And his lovely Hindl had to live with cheap, hideous things. Could he have borne to bring her to a home filled with stuff that was already broken down and worthless? Could he bear to have her work with a burnt-out, half-cracked kitchen stove, or rest in an old bumpy bed that left her broken in the morning, or give her the added agony of making shift with unsteady table, or half-broken chairs?

I sympathized with his eagerness to give my mother the best he could get, but I dreaded the Installment Plan Agent. My mother must have known the devotion, the passion that drove him into debt for her. "But Israel," she would plead, "don't buy anything more, this way. You see that we can't live, as it is."

My step-father's gains were uncertain. Some days he'd clear two or three or three and a half dollars. On other days there would be no gains at all. There would even be losses through a bad "buy." Or he would be cheated in the sale of his load. On such days the horse had to get his feed as when he salvaged two or three dollars from his labor. I brought home little enough, that first winter: between one and two dollars a week, at first. After that, from two and a half to three and a half dollars a week; and toward the end of the winter nearer four.

Food became so scarce in our cupboard that we almost measured out every square inch of bread. There was nothing left for clothing and shoes. I wore mine till the snow and slush came through. I had often to sit all day at my bench with icy feet in wet leather. My dress was worn to a threadbareness that brought me the jibes of some of my shopmates. I confided this to my mother. She looked about the barren rooms and wrung her hands, but said nothing. My mother knew my need for a frock—had known it for a long time. But how get me one? Well, that week she'd try. But that week was worse than the week before.

Something however must be got; anything—something that will make a dress!

Returning from work one evening, I found my mother at the kitchen table working on a bit of new checkered gingham. It was a frock for me. On a day when the sidewalks were solid ice under a blanket of new snow I first wore my gay little gingham dress. Over it was my thin jacket, clutched close with numb fingers. And I was working ten or eleven hours a day with swift, sure hands. Mr. Wertheim had said, one morning: "Rose Pastor, you're the quickest and best worker in the shop!" I didn't know or think how much I was earning for Mr. Wertheim, but I knew I was getting hunger and cold for my portion.

All winter long I wore the gingham dress and thin jacket. Every morning of that winter, when my mother tucked my lunch of bread and milk and an apple—or orange—or banana—newspaper-wrapped under my arm and opened the door to let me out into the icy dawn, I felt the agony that tugged at her mother-heart. "Walk fast," she would always say, "walk as fast as you can, Rosalie. Remember, it is better to walk fast in the cold."

After the long day in the stogie factory, and after supper and the chores for mother, there was my book—there were Lamb's *Tales*—the magic of words . . . Before the kitchen stove, when the house was asleep, I'd throw off my shoes, thaw out the icy tissues that bit all day into my consciousness, and lose myself in the loves and losses, the sorrows and joys, the gore-dripping tragedies and gay comedies of kings and queens, lords and ladies of olden times. I read and re-read the "Tales" with never-flagging interest. But (and this is perhaps a noteworthy fact) with complete detachment. Not then, nor later, when I read Shakespeare in the text did I ever, for even a fleeting moment identify myself with the people of Shakespeare's dramas. The rich lords and ladies, the ruling kings and queens of whom the supreme dramatist wrote in such noble strain, were alien to me. They moved in a different world. On the other hand, there lurked in my heart an undefined feeling of resentment over the fact that his clowns were always poor folk. He seemed never to draw a poor man save to make him an object of ridicule. Instinctively, I identified myself with his poor. Years later when I came in contact with the Baconian Theory I was naturally inclined to accept it. Lord Bacon could not have viewed the servants and slaves of his class and his period in any other light. But Shakespeare—"the lowly lad of Avon"—who was arrested for poaching on a rich man's preserves!—I held it against him in a vague, unformed way that he, poor too, could elect to make of his own kind, clouts and clowns, *Bobbees* and *Bottoms*, butts for the mirth of the wealthy patrons of the Elizabethan theatre.

During my first year in America I read nothing but Lamb's "Tales." I had nothing else to read, looked for nothing else. It never occurred to me that there might be other books in the world. I had never heard of any. In the stillness of night I would read softly but audibly to myself from between the dull-red covers of my sole treasure.

◆ ◆ ◆

At the end of winter I had quit the shop under the viaduct, and Spring found me in Mr. Brudno's "factory." Mr. Brudno ran what cigar-makers in Ohio called a "buckeye." A "buckeye" is a cigar "factory" in a private home. In other words, it was a sweat shop.

In the three small rooms that comprised Mr. Brudno's stogie "factory" were a dozen scattered benches. Of the dozen workers at the bench not counting strippers, bookers, and packers, six were Brudno's very own: four sons and two daughters. Several others were blood-relations—first cousins; and still another was a distant connection by marriage. The remaining few were "outsiders"; young girls and boys and—I—came to fill the last unoccupied bench.

Mr. Brudno was a picturesque patriarch, with his long black beard, and his tall black skull-cap.[2] He had come from the old country with a little money (not acquired through toil, rumor had it) and was deter-mined to get rich quick in America. With money and six grown chil-dren, and the persuasive need of his poverty-stricken relatives and com-patriots here and in the old world, he had an undoubted advantage over the rest of us. He put his children to work, and drew in his poor rela-tions. In this godless America he would give them plenty of work in a shop where the Sabbath was kept holy! It was his strength, for they would work in no shop where the Sabbath was not kept holy. Their learner's period to be stretched out far beyond the usual time limit, thus adding much to his profits. The "outsiders" were young children. He hired them and drove them, and kept reducing their pay.

He would go about the "buckeye" dreaming aloud . . . This was his first sweatshop. By-and-bye he'd have a bigger place—a real stogie fac-tory with dozens of new workers. His children would do all the work of foremen and watchers, and work at the bench too. Soon there would be a big factory building all his own. . . .

In the six years, off and on, that I worked for Mr. Brudno, his dream grew to reality. He did everything a boss could do to make his dream come true. Beginning in a little "buckeye," he soon moved to an enormous loft, where the dozen benches he started with, were many times multiplied. There his factory hummed with the industry of boys and girls, of men, women, and young children. The stripping and the bunch-making were concentrated in one end of the vast room where the rolling was done. The raw material was unpacked and sorted, the drying, storing, and other processes carried on in another room. Driven by Mr. Brudno and our own need, we piled up stogies rapidly. Brudno paid miserably little for our labor, and always complained that we were getting too much. But before long, he was able to rear a factory building of his own, on a very desirable site on Broadway. It was of red brick— and several stories high. There he drove us harder than ever, and in time added another story to his Broadway structure. Now he was a big "manufacturer"; he strutted about and watched us manufacture.

The Brudno family lived in a large house on Orange Street now. From their windows at a fork in the road where the street flowed into Broadway, they could see the factory—the source of all good things. . . .

Soon, his children underwent a remarkable change. They dressed differently from the rest of us, and looked with scorn upon our poor clothing, and our poor lives. They were getting culture. They discussed art, literature and the theatre with each other as they moved about the rest of us, and rarely deigned to draw any of us into their discussions. They were no longer tied to the work-bench, but came and went as they liked. Their occupations were pleasant now, and varied. After all, were they not the sons and daughters of the boss? . . . The cleavage became sharper, from day to day.

One of Mr. Brudno's six children, a swarthy young son, was sent to college.[3] He attended Yale, and studied Greek and Latin among other marvelous things. Today his name graces the door to a successful lawyer's office somewhere in Cleveland.

At the age of twelve I had the good fortune to "fall in love" with this homely lad. I say "good fortune" because the circumstances were such as to provide me with a wholesome influence at a time when I was just awakening—and in need of a firm devotion. We were really strangers from start to finish. In those six years, and two beyond of my enchantment, we had three "conversations." The first—perhaps shortest, strangest speech in lovers' history—was when I rushed from my bench with other workers at the news of a street accident, and came to one of the windows. There stood Zelig! Of course, I was rooted to the spot! I could not go forward nor turn back and run. He had then been for a week or more the bright object of my deep devotion. But I could as soon have hoped to hitch my step-father's literal wagon to a literal star, as to have touched his hand. A young worker had remarked to me in the shop, one day: "Look at Zelig in that new hat. Becoming, isn't it?" At this, never before having looked at any being in any hat, I had promptly "fallen in love." It seemed to me that I had never beheld a being so glorious as that swarthy lugubrious youth! So, when the creature of my dreams turned from the window and looked at me I could move neither hand nor foot. Then—out of his four or five years greater maturity and riper wisdom, he shattered the spell of my embarrassment by making talk. As he addressed himself to me, an unbearable tightness gripped my throat. My idol placed one hand in his coat pocket, the other on his heart, thumb caught in vest, and murmured the unforgettable question:

"So you like noodle-pudding?"

"Yes," I blurted; and my tongue having at that moment released my legs, I turned and ran.

That was our first "conversation." Our second, a year-and-a-half or two years later, took place when he asked me the time of day from his cousin's work-bench at the far end of the loft on Broadway. Looking up at the clock on the wall—where I could see it and he couldn't—I told him. It was some minutes past two, I remember; and how thrilled I was that he had asked *me*!

A long time had again passed before we had our third and last "conversation." What it was I no longer recall. We passed each other on the stairs. He would have said "good morning," or something of equal importance, and I would have muttered some monosyllable and stumbled up- or downstairs, as the case would have been.

Until my twentieth year the dream held—a dream based upon ambition to learn: He loved books! He possessed and read books! And books were my passion too. . . . That was the secret of his hold on my imagination.

I steeped myself in books.

◆ ◆ ◆

"Look," Brudno would say, "if she can do it, why can't you and you do it—and you? Earn more! You need to, don't you?"

Yes—*need!*—we understood that force well.

The workers at Brudno's would race with me, and gradually increase their speed. And I would race with the clock—and further increase my own . . .

By summer's end, I was the pride of Brudno's heart. I sped up the others, and turned out again as many stogies as the average slow ones. He was seeing results.

When the "buckeye" moved to the big loft and became a factory, Mr. Brudno announced a cut. The stogie-rollers were getting fourteen cents a hundred. Now it would be thirteen. We took the cut in silence. We were for the most part poor little child slaves, timid and unorganized. The thought of union never occurred to us. There was no strength in us or behind us. It was each one by his lone self. Not one of us would have ventured to pit his little self against the boss. We merely looked into one another's faces. No words. But each had the same thought in mind: Now there would be less of something that was already scarce: Bread, milk, or coal. Mr. Brudno owned the factory and we were his workers.

Nothing could be done about it. So we raced some more . . . and still more, and more!

It never occurred to me that I was being used by the boss to set the pace in his stogie factory . . . And that one cut would follow another, as our speed increased . . .

A cut came the week that the new baby came.

"Rosalie!"

My step-father's voice, tense and unnatural with excitement, shook me out of sleep.

I heard my mother's shriek piercing the deep night, and rushed into the room next to mine.

"Mother! Oh, my mother!" What could be wrong with my mother?

My step-father rushed after me, and snatched me out of the room.

"Rosalie, run to the midwife! Say she's to come right away. Mother's giving birth. Quick!"

"Giving birth?" A new baby coming! . . . Out into the dark, chill, deserted streets I went, shoes unbuttoned, hair loose in the wind, feet flying . . .

It was hard enough to scrape together the ten dollars for the midwife. To get help for the two weeks of confinement was out of the question. For those two weeks, after shop, I did the work at home. There was no water in the flat on Liberal Street. I had to carry pails of water from the pump in the yard to fill the wash tubs upstairs and take the water down to spill. How heavy the sheets were, and how hard to rub clean! . . . Every day of the two weeks, I washed: Diapers, sheets, other "linens," carrying water up and down, up and down, till all was washed and rinsed, and the white things hanging out on the line in the yard.

There were meals to get and dishes to wash, my two-year-old brother to care for, and special things to prepare for my mother. Mornings, be-fore daylight, my step-father would make the fire, and I would get the breakfast. He would stay to wash up the dishes and do a few chores before starting for his horse and wagon and the struggle with another day. By noon, the ailing Mrs. Feinberg would look in on my mother and babies and help out a bit. For those two weeks, I was given the privilege of leaving an hour earlier daily, on my own time of course, to help my mother.

At night, with tired feet and hands, and heaviness that hung on my eyelids and threatened to close them, I'd take up *Les Miserables* and shed a few hot tears of sympathy for poor little Cosette! . . .

• • •

There were now five mouths to feed. My step-father tried desperately to supply bread for his growing family. He worked early and late. When winter came again, there were days when he'd climb down from his wagon with difficulty. The everlong exposure to frost and winter storm, and his attempt to save by taking no food during the day, began to tell on his splendid strength. He grew haggard and troubled. Deep lines ran like large new moons along the sides of his cheeks. There were lines like wires across his forehead. He was unable to understand why, with such hard trying, he could not keep hunger shut out; why he could not drive the stubborn wolf from the door!

I was then in my thirteenth year. Already I felt the staggering weight of the struggle upon my shoulders. I worked all day. My fingers flew! But what I got, together with what my hardworking step-father got, was not enough to keep us in the bare, needed things.

One day I had an idea. That evening after supper I slipped on my coat. My mother protested.

"Where are you going? And the dishes?"

"I'll do them when I get back."

My step-father protested. "Such a young child should not run around in the evenings." And my mother, musing on it, said, "well, Israel, she's growing up. She'll be wanting some pleasure, poor child mine! She has little enough—nothing but her books! And these when she should sleep and rest. I suppose you're going over to Ida's house. . . . Let her go, Israel, let her go. It may be more cheerful there than here."

It was the same for several evenings, till I came home with the glad news.

"Mother! father! I've found one—where I didn't think to look: right here on Liberal Street, in the middle of the block!"

I had followed clues, night after night, but nothing had come of them. And here, on our very own street—by chance—in crossing to the other side, I discovered a "buckeye" tucked away in the rear of a yard. I had walked in, found the "boss" at his own bench, and asked for evening work. And he had said, "Come tomorrow, after supper."

How happy I was! At last I could help more.

But my mother drew me to her, kissed me and cried, and insisted that I must not go: "It is bad enough that you have to slave ten or eleven hours a day, and then do things about the house. How can I let you work all day and all night too! Was it to such a fate as this we were born?" My step-father went about the room beating his breast in silence. Then he broke into angry protest. "Damn such a life—damn, damn."

They threatened to lock me in, evenings. I threatened to take no supper and go from the factory direct to the "buckeye."

The following evening, my parents exchanged glances as we sat at table, so I rushed up from supper, bolted through the door, coatless, and ran down the street. I would have lost my chance to work had I failed to turn up as agreed.

All that winter, after the long day at Brudno's, I rolled stogies till midnight in the little "buckeye," lively as a sparrow because I was doing my utmost to help.

• • •

In the Spring that followed, Jennie's mother died, and the Feinberg family moved away.

"It is easier bringing water in and out on the ground floor," said my step-father. "A healthier place for the baby," thought my mother. So we moved into the rooms where the Feinbergs had lived. The thin floors with no cellar under them proved cold and damp. Spring brought much illness to our little world, and the baby took sick. Then too, my mother was nursing him at the breast, not knowing that she was with child again. The Doctor came and examined the infant. "You are poisoning him with your milk," he said. "Influenza is in the air."

For eight long months, without relief, my mother hovered over her baby. She barely slept, snatching an hour only when I was there to take her place at the side of the cradle. At first it was one lung, then double pneumonia. My step-father took a loan to pay the doctor; mortgaged his horse and wagon to bring him to the child. At the end of those eight gruelling months, the third baby, my sister Lily, was born.

Pale and spent, with her dark head listless against the pillows, my mother lay with a child on each arm; the new-born infant and the newly-rescued infant. There was not a year between them, and both needed her every moment of the day and a good part of the disturbed night. Little Maurice, the eldest, not yet four, clung to a white hand on the coverlet, and gazed gravely at his mother and the two equally helpless infants . . .

We were now a family of six.

How to make ends meet?

My mother, my step-father, and I would figure to the minutest fraction the possible saving in this or that kind of food. Soup-bones, cabbage, stale bread—"a cent cheaper than the fresh, and better at that!" But no matter how we figured, we couldn't cover our need. Eggs and milk for the little ones, however, that we would have.

And again winter was coming. I must find another "buckeye"—must take evening work again. The boss was beginning to dismiss workers. More empty work-benches gaped ominously each morning at those of us who were still employed.

Something was in the air. Not only at Brudno's, but everywhere. Our little world of working fathers, dependent mothers, and young bread-winners was tense with an apprehension never felt before.

We were always hanging over a precipice. But now we felt that something was going to break; that the precarious bit of shale we called "life" to which we clung in such desperation would give way; and that we— all of us—with our poverty and our crust of bread, would go crashing down to disaster! This was the beginning of the crisis of 1893.

My step-father, though no worker in a factory, felt the effects of the crisis along with the rest of our class. His horse and wagon now carried fewer and fewer of the loads that gave a precarious living. At the week's end, after all was paid—feed and stall for the horse and shed-rent for the wagon—he would find only four or five dollars clear.

He worked harder now and cleared less. He would bring his diminishing loads to the warehouses, and get smaller return for them with every passing day. A deep depression settled upon him.

My own work too fell off. Most of the workers at Brudno's were sent home. A few were kept on part-time. These were the quickest and best workers—the most profitable to him in busy season—the boss preferred not to lose them. He pretended to be generous in keeping us on the payroll.

The three or three-and-a-half dollars I brought, when added to the miserable little that my poor step-father was able to bring in, spelled deeper need for us.

• • •

"Father, what's the matter? You're not eating *anything* these days."

"It's all right, Rosalie. I'll eat tomorrow."

He would go off into the bitter winter dawns without tasting food.

He seemed to be hurrying; now more than ever; always hurrying—as though trying to catch up with and overtake a rapidly vanishing hope of survival.

At night he would return and sit dejected at the table, never touching his supper.

"Israel, take a potato and a piece of herring," my mother would urge, placing a cheek against his cheek.

"Come, eat something. You can't starve yourself altogether because times are bitter. It will do none of us any good. You make it hard for the rest of us to eat our crust when you won't take a bit of it. Come!"

I see him in tears—see him break down and weep like a little child, his strong frame shaken with his sobbing.

"Take a quarter, every day, and buy yourself some good lunch, Israel," my mother begged.

But how could he spend a quarter—a whole quarter a day for lunch? His horse must have feed, his wife and children must have bread, and there was so little for his labor . . . And the crisis deepened.

One evening, some time later, my mother unburdened her troubled heart to me.

"I'm afraid, Rosalie, I'm afraid. Israel is going to the saloon for free lunches. He buys a beer to get a bite to eat. The bitterest days he goes in to get warm. He saves a few nickels on food, but where will it lead?"

I tried to quiet her fears.

"Soon father will be earning more. Then maybe he can buy lunches in a decent place."

But I was troubled. And again I began a long search for evening work. Finally, I found a "buckeye" some distance from home, where I was given work for two evenings a week. It was not much, but it was something. I ran home with the hopeful tidings.

When I came to the door, I stopped. My heart beat violently. I saw my gentle, generous step-father, turned half brute with drink, struggling with my mother. My mother in agonized tones was pleading with him. I hurried in and slammed the door shut.

"Father," I called sharply. "You're drunk!"

He turned from my mother, and lurched toward me.

"So!—so you too call me names!"

Before I could escape, he had struck me a heavy blow across the face.

"That's all right, father, I won't call you names."

With quiet talk, I got him to his cot. I drew off his shoes and his coat, and covered him with a blanket. He muttered unintelligible things, and fell asleep . . . Soon the air was fetid with his breath.

Maurice, the eldest, cried and clung to his mother. The baby sister in the cradle was crying and little Emmanuel, the rescued one, wailed weakly. It was long before he could cry like any other child.

It took time to quiet them and get them to sleep.

Then my mother came and stood over the man she loved.

"Better to have died! Better to have died!" she moaned. She would not go to bed, but wailed and talked to herself far into the night. I sat beside her, filled with a great grief, but my eyes were dry. Endlessly there would be nights with scenes like this, but I did not foresee them. I felt only the tragedy of the moment.

"Go to sleep now, Mamele."

But she would not.

"What do you know, child, oh, what do you know!"

As we sat there and talked, however, a little I began to realize that, hereafter, added to poverty and hunger and the mad struggle to survive, would be the decay of that which was still sweet and sound at the kernel of life. A blind brute force, raging and relentless, had entered our home to stay. It would tear at the vitals of her children, at her love, and at the sound fabric of the man she loved.

But only a little of all this I comprehended. I was fourteen; not old enough to realize the full force of our disaster.

Now we went through that winter of crisis and tragedy—on what we subsisted; of the days of stark hunger; of the endless trudgings from one closed factory to another; of our struggle with my poor step-father giving himself over more to drink, the more his hope of livelihood vanished; of the nights without sleep because of hunger and despair; of the days in a frozen flat; of the children who cried for bread in the cold . . . I cannot tell of them now. There are some things in the lives of the workers that cannot be told. We have no words in which to tell them, even to each other in secret. These things, I feel, must lie buried in the hearts of our class, till they find expression in our deeds—on the great day of our self-emancipation.

• • •

We had a spell of temporary relief. Someone was willing to be a boarder.

How hard we tried to make shift in the already crowded quarters, the cheerless rooms whose cold air made grey mist of our warm breaths! How my mother struggled to serve him! I too, giving every spare moment of my time. Himself a poor worker he paid so very little, but we hoped it would help us to catch up a bit with the rent. Maybe then the landlord would not carry out his threat to dispossess us.

We didn't keep our boarder long. He was an unwholesome man, and I was glad when he was gone, though it meant the street for our few belongings. Where could we go with not a penny to advance on rent?

I went to Mr. Brudno with many misgivings and begged him for an advance in order to have a deposit on rent. He bargained much, cautioning me to remember when busy season came again, not to leave him for another boss. He advanced me ten dollars.

We moved in a blizzard. A tiny frame house stood vacant on the next lot, at Number Two Liberal Street. We gathered up the babies and moved into that tiny frame house, giving part payment on a month's rent. We lugged our few scattered belongings through a blinding, raging snow storm, sending the stove first—glad that we had found a way out so close at hand.

In the back of the new yard was an old shed. Here my step-father housed his horse and wagon and saved on shed-rent.

It gave him hope again.

"Look here, Mamele," he said with cheer, "it will help a lot. Now I shall be able to make a living."

He made a new start—tried to keep out of the saloon.

"Now we'll manage if I earn a little more—just a little more." How glad he was! But the force that held millions of the working class in a relentless grip of compulsory idleness and starvation was stronger than the strongest individual among us. A living was simply not to be made.

Though a man threw his heart and his hands and his whole being into the battle for bread, those millions that were doomed were doomed! . . . A weaker man would have taken gas. He took alcohol.

"Father," I begged, "try! See if you can't keep away. If you tried hard enough, maybe . . ."

"I'll try, Rosalie. Did I hurt you yesterday? I'm sorry; you know I'm sorry. Mamele, come here." And he'd put an arm about my poor tormented mother; "You know what's in my heart. Do I want to hurt you, or her?"

My mother knew! He had a heart of gold. He would have had that heart cut up into little bits to feed his children. He was not to blame. Something else was to blame. He did not know what. My mother did not know what. Something without a name. It was stronger than the strongest man. No man could struggle against it when it had him in its grip. And men in the grip of this thing took their lives, or turned to crime, or to drink—because there seemed no other way out.

"Yes, Israel; yes, I know. Only, for the sake of the children . . ."

But the deepening crisis was too much for him. My mother saw the man she loved, the father of her children, descend to depths of misery and defeat from which there would be no returning.

• • •

The time came again when every bench was occupied—when the face of the clock was again the face of a foe.

Mr. Brudno was often in a genial mood now, but not too often. Frequently he was morose; at times, vindictive. His black skull-cap announced the mood. If he came through the swinging doors with the cap to his right or left ear we expected taciturnity or jest. If the cap sat against the back of his skull we looked for trouble. Then no work he examined was good enough for him. He would go from rack to rack; picking up handfuls of stogies. A mis-roll or two, a head or two badly sealed; a slight unevenness in length would call forth a violent fit of temper. He would hurl curses at the workers, break and twist the stogies out of shape, and throw them into the drawer of waste cuttings! A morning's work gone to the scrap-pile!

"You call this stogie-rolling? Get out of my shop. Get out, this minute, or I'll pitch you through the window."

Perhaps there were a couple of hundred of stogies left in the rack. The worker was not always allowed to take them down, or count them. Cowed, pale with fear she would leave the loft in silence. The rest of us, bending our heads close to the work, were set to thinking—thoughts differing widely, feeling running from white fear to red rebellion—as after-mutterings revealed.

The most intolerable fines were inflicted upon us. For example, the leaf tobacco in which we rolled our "bunches" was often so rotted that we were forced to re-roll our stogies several times, each time removing the worthless piece to try another. Or, the leaf would be so badly worm-eaten we could not cover a third of the required number of stogies. This bad stock retarded the work. It meant rolling two or three hundred less in a day; it meant beside, unusual effort; increased care and anxiety; and a nervous strain that sent us home trembling from head to feet. Yet for this stock Mr. Brudno demanded the same standard of workmanship and the same number of stogies to the pound that was set for the finest leaf tobacco, and docked us heavily for the inescapable failure. When we opened our slim pay envelopes, we would often find from fifty cents to one dollar and fifty cents deducted, out of a possible five dollars. When driven too hard, some one of us would venture to complain in a timid voice: "But look at this stock, Mr. Brudno. How can you expect the same work out of such rotten leaf tobacco? See this and this and this!—and look at the holes in these . . . Look! look! I just brought this pound from the stripping room. We can't do the impossible!"

"Well, what's wrong with this stock anyway? A little hole, here and there—that's nothing. Rotten? That ain't rotten. You pull too hard, so it tears. Don't pull, or you'll go home."

"Ask your own sons and daughters; they'll tell you what sort of stock it is."

But if he ever asked them we were not told. The fines were taken out of our pay often without any previous warning; and those who complained too disrespectfully were "fired."

If a period of good stock followed, we would race madly. Now is the time to make up for the bad weeks! If then we succeeded—if we increased our speed and turned out a few hundred stogies more than usual at the week's end, Mr. Brudno would announce a reduction of a cent or two on the hundred. Before these attacks we were helpless sheep. We knew nothing of organizing protest. A few of us dreamed . . . But nothing came of our dreams.

Brudno's shop, however, was to have a strike—a curious strike confined to his relatives. One morning, at daybreak, I was roused by a sharp rap at our door. It was Lyoti, one of that group of blood relations whom Brudno drew from the old country with tales of work and freedom, in a shop that kept the Sabbath holy.

"I came to beg you please, not to go back to the shop, this morning!" he said, "We are on strike."

"We? Who?"

"The boss's relations," he explained. "We can't do the special work he gives us to do, and live on the pay. It is impossible."

I roused my sleeping mother. The children woke. They ran or toddled to the door of the tiny frame house on Orange Street where we now lived; half-naked; sleepy, yet curious.

I kissed my mother, kissed each child in turn, and forgot for the moment that our father, in despair, had left home the week before and had not been heard from since. A strike at Brudno's shop! Every outraged feeling in me broke into exultant rebellion.

"I'll stay out even if we starve altogether! Eh, Mamele?" My mother kissed me and nodded assent. There were shadows as we contemplated the children. "But a strike is a strike," said my mother. And Lyoti explained, "If we win you win too. If we win the boss will not dare to press you harder than he is already pressing you. He will not dare to take another cent off the hundred from anybody."

My first strike—a sympathy strike! I visited workers in their homes that early morning and got them to stay out. I picketed the shop. Lyoti turned to me for many strike activities. I did as directed and drew in others. At the end of some ten or twelve days the men returned in triumph. The boss had yielded to their demands, and the rest of us who appeared to have gained nothing, felt stronger—even a bit audacious in the presence of the boss. The old timidity never again quite overcame any of us—for was he not beaten in our sight?

Lyoti had a fine tenor voice, and knew many folk and art songs, as well as airs from the operas and complete movements from the works of great composers. Lyoti became my loyal friend, and taught me many of the songs he knew. When he asked me to marry him, I solemnly confessed to him that my heart was with his cousin Zelig. And though he proposed to me every six months or so over a period of seven years, each time forgetting his promise to be "just good friends," it did not spoil our friendship. We agreed to be hopelessly in love, each in his own way. He learned many new songs for my sake, and I read many books for Zelig's sake. We were happy in our misery and our company.

• • •

"What are you doing, Rosalie!" my mother cried out and clapped her hands over her ears as if trying to keep out a shrieking sound.

"My God! child, we haven't slept under this roof yet. Why are you tearing down the walls already?" I tried to stop her, but she continued. "We haven't paid the rent yet. Do you want the landlord to throw us into the street the first day we come in?"

The rent . . . the landlord . . . the street . . .

Want—the Giant that strode in seven-league boots through our lean pay-envelopes, like famine through a drought-stricken land, forced us to look for cheaper quarters. My step-father had loaded his wagon and moved the family in the early morning, and I had come home from work to find—this! The concealed effrontery of all the ugliness that poverty had ever forced upon us challenged me in the form of the most hideous wallpaper ever invented!

The place we had moved from had a kitchen painted a Paris-green. Walls and ceiling—Paris-green. My hours at home were spent in the kitchen, and those Paris-green walls and ceiling tormented me. I could not read, could not think surrounded by them. To this green hell we have moved from a flat that had one tiny room whose walls were a neutral tint—a restful haven that was a place to escape to, away from the cook-stove and the clambering children. The tint had been applied who knows what ages ago! But the walls were gentle and unobtrusive. In the Paris-green kitchen I yearned for that tiny room. The factory sapped me of strength. I needed rest, and the green kitchen was a torment. I could not ask the family to move on that account. But at the end of three months Want became my ally. Cheaper rooms were found. They would be nicely papered, said the landlord, and we could move in on the First. My step-father did the moving in the early morning hours, as usual. From work I hurried to the new home with a singing heart, only to be confronted by this last word in ugliness—this monstrous wallpaper in hideous contortions of red and green and gold! In revolt against the insult I had assailed the paper, pried loose strip after strip with my finger-nails, brought it down, band after band.

"Don't stop me, Mamele," I cried, "don't stop me!" Something in my voice checked her. She paused, hand raised, motionless. We both remained silent. Only the paper shrieked as I brought it down—as I laid the monster of ugliness low with ten relentless fingers. Then sobs came from an exultant throat. I was glad! Let the landlord do what he will. Behind the paper was a restful wall. Why couldn't he have left it like that? Then I sank into a chair and wept and wept! My mother stole quietly out of the room.

Amid the clutter of household goods, the few rickety possessions, acquired on the Installment Plan and long since become unfit for proper use, I sat and wept until dusk came. Then I dropped head and arms on a packing-case half-filled with odds and ends, and shut out ugliness. I had need to invoke the few visions of peace, light, sweetness that memory reconstructed magically from childhood days. They were still close to my sixteen years, and they came back on bright wings. Wide waters of a Mazurian lake. A fisherman's boat. The face of my grandfather reflecting kindness as the waters reflected light. The sound of the keel on the shining stillness. The rhythmical oars, the brown net through the silver waters, the iridescent fleet life in the marshes. And a child's heart near to breaking with joy and wonder . . . A bird singing-flying in the tall rafters and singing. High windows open to the sun, a bird flying sunward. A heart thrilling to the bird's note, to the bird's flight . . . Goodbye, little town of Augustova! Goodbye, thatched-roof cottage; goodbye to town well, goodbye, girl with the shining red hair. Goodbye, beloved grandfather Berl. The stage flies. The two horses are two wings that will never fly back for them they bear away . . . Suddenly the little child grows conscious of night and stars . . . The stage stops on the Prussian border. The passengers alight. They go into a sleepy inn for a cup of *tchai* and a bun. It is not yet dawn. The drowsy inn-keeper serves the *tchai* in silence. But what is this the little me is tasting of? A bun? There never was such a flavor in all the world!

The sixteen-year-old me with head on packing-case stirs a bit. After eight years in the squalid East End of London, and five in the suffocating atmosphere of American tobacco factories the taste of that bun remains unforgettable. Once, in a London bakeshop window I saw a bun that bore a tantalizing resemblance to that morsel; small, wonderfully round, light as a breath, with a delicate sprinkling of powdered white sugar, white and finer than any I had ever seen in London Town before. Breathless, I had hurried home to my Aunt Sarah and begged her to buy me one of those buns. But oh, the disappointment! It was only an ordinary bun—the haunting flavor was not there! Frustrated, I had cried aloud. As I lay with head on arms, conjuring up the few precious moments my childhood had known the flavor of the bun eaten at dawn in the sleepy inn came back to me and filled me with a yearning not born of the palate. Memory of taste and touch, sound, sight and smell of all things good and beautiful and sweet that I had known to the age of three returned to me and touched me with its medicinal touch. I fell asleep. In the morning I found myself on the floor, upon a mattress where my mother had placed me. Our brazen chanticleer, the alarm clock, perched on a bread-box near my head, awakened me to the reality of factory toil, and to the unbearable paper that still hung in a few tattered banners on the wall I had attacked.

"Mother," I pleaded, "if the landlord won't give us decent paper we'll move right out again, yes?"

"Yes," said my understanding mother, on her brow a pucker, on her lips a smile.

• • •

There was much singing in the shop, and many voices. But I fell into the role of shop soloist. These times when the boss went through the loft on his punitive expeditions and left a trail of hot rebelliousness behind him someone would call out: "Sing, Rose, sing!" And I would break into one or another of the many songs I had gathered from various sources:

Tyrants, you cannot compel us!
Doomed is your tyranny.
We'll triumph despite you—we'll triumph.
Till all the world shall be free . . .

There were many songs like this, with many verses. At the end of each verse, the whole shop would repeat the last line. If the boss's sons and daughters knew what we were singing and why, they gave no sign.

There were favorite songs. "Sing, Rose, sing 'My Testament,'" and I would sing that song of Edelstadt's, more poignant with mourning than fiery with revolt:

Ah, good friends, when I am gone,
Bring our flag to my grave.
The free flag, the red one,
Dyed in the blood of workingmen.

There in my grave will I hear
My free song, my storm song

And there will I shed tears
For the enslaved Gentile and Jew.

And when I hear the swords ring
In the last conflict of blood and pain,
To the folk of the grave will I sing
And inspire even dead hearts.[4]

My songs were not always songs of rebellion. There were hymns and the popular ballads of the time, old ballads, and folk songs of many nations; especially the Scotch of which I knew very many; airs from the operas; and the classical German lieder. But labor songs and songs of revolt had a special place in our hearts. They were the only expression of protest at hand. I sang as I came up the stairs in the morning, and sang as I left the loft at night. The boss would often hear me singing, but he seemed never to know what it was about. At times, he would stop, shove his skull-cap over an ear, and ask: "How is it with the wind-pipe? Does it never tire?" "Never, never!" I would fling back gaily. Once I found some verses—tore them out of a story-book that my step-father had in a sack on the wagon. In a fever of excitement I had made a melody for it, and brought the new song to the shop. I recall but one verse and the refrain:

How little do the great ones care
Who are at home secure
What hidden dangers colliers dare,
What hardships they endure?
The bright fire their mansions boast
To cheer themselves and wives,
Mayhap were kindled at the cost
Of jovial colliers' lives—

Down in a coal mine
Underneath the ground
Where a gleam of sunshine
Is never to be found.

Digging dusky diamonds
All the season round
Down in a coal mine underneath the ground.

Not great poetry; but for me it contained a great message. I had never heard about miners until I read those verses. I looked upon coal with new eyes.

• • •

"Nat, why do you wear such thick glasses?"

"My eyes are bad," said Nat.

"What made 'em?"

"Reading," said Nat.

"Reading?" I looked up, eager. That was my passion, too. "What do you read?" I asked.

"Socialism," said Nat.

"Socialism? What's that?"

"Have you never heard of Socialism?"

"Never. What is it?"

Nat talked, from time to time looking about him to make sure that the boss was not there. He told us of a man by the name of Karl Marx—a name, he said, that was sacred to the working class. For Karl Marx showed the workers how they will some day abolish poverty.

"Poverty, and misery, and insecurity," said Nat, "are not things that a cruel God put into the world to punish us for our sins. Poverty and all its evils can be abolished, and the workers will some day abolish them through Socialism."

"Have you heard of the poet Shelley?" asked Nat.

"Yes, I've read some of his poems. Was he a Socialist?"

"You'd think so," Nat said, "if you'd read certain of his poems." And he quoted passage after fiery passage. I was flamed inwardly when he declaimed:

Rise like lions after slumber
In unvanquishable number!

Shake your chains to earth like dew
Which in sleep had fall'n on you!
Ye are many, they are few.

How long the time seemed before I could leave the shop and carry the message to my mother!

"Mamele, Mamele," I cried as I burst into the house that evening, "It isn't true that poverty will always be in the world just because it always has been! No! We workers will abolish poverty. When the workers of all lands unite . . ." And without stopping to take breath I told her what I had heard from Nat, that day. As we sat over our meagre supper, the children—wan, wide-eyed, listened to a new interpretation of their pinched pale faces, their empty plates, their emptier futures unless . . . unless . . . as if my burning new words were not all pure fiery sound to them—except possibly to the eldest, who was in his eighth year.

No need to suffer poverty! What a world-shattering idea! Not inevitable—poverty! We the Many, they the Few . . . "We—we the workers will change it all some day." Hope—there was hope in the world . . . Nevertheless, it was passed on to me as vague notion: Vote . . . organize . . . solidarity . . . workers of all countries, unite . . . How? . . . When? . . . Yet the seed was planted. It sang in the soil that was me, the worker.

Hitherto, my vision had turned upon a blank wall: no way out—none. Strikes? Yes, of that I had some notion. Strikes—for a little more wages, a shorter work-day, better shop conditions. But these things we would strike for, always. Change—great change? That thought never occurred to me. Every problem born of our poverty brought with it a sense of impotence: No escape, no help, anywhere!

I knew only one word of appeal: "Oh God, Oh God, Oh God!" A vast vague nebulous Somebody to whom the helpless poor raised helpless hands. A chance paper, picked up in the streets years ago had brought to me the Church's philosophy of Jesus: Turn The Other Cheek. In a certain sense and to a certain extent I was dominated by those ideas.

A social rebel—a rebel against anything that afflicted or oppressed my class, or me or mine as members of my class, I was nevertheless a non-resistant in "personal" matters and turned the other cheek in individual disputes. I called upon God when aches or pains or weariness or other personal cares beset me. So strong was this spirit of meekness in me that I would have carried it much further had not life and the struggle forced ever new aspects of rebelliousness on me. But after Nat talked, though the old cry of God God God broke from my lips often enough, I never again uttered it without the electrifying thought coming after: "And there need not be poverty any more!"

◆ ◆ ◆

Six of the twelve years that I spent in the cigar factories of Cleveland were spent, off and on, at Brudno's. The rest were scattered over many shops: Baer Brothers, Feder Brothers, and many whose names I no longer recall. Once when my mother urged a change, I tried work in a shirt-waist factory. But I could not bear the din of the electric sewing machines. Evening after evening I would return from work to throw myself upon my cot in a fit of weeping. If the effluvium of tobacco dust was an evil, the unceasing roar of the machines was a greater evil. It made speech with a fellow-worker impossible. It drowned out the sound of singing, and swallowed up whatever was *me* in tidal waves of incredible noise. At the end of two months I was back in the cigar factory. At another time, when my speed broke—, when, try as I might, I could not make my hitherto remarkably swift fingers do more than creep over my work, I left the cigar factory again. For ten months I worked in Mr. Black's department store on Ontario Street. I stood on my feet all day and on Saturday till ten in the evening, selling ladies bonnets . . . Again I went back to the cigar factory.

With the monopoly of the newly-invented suction machine, by which a worker could turn out many times the number of cigars made by skilled hand labor, the Cigar Trust came into existence. It was spreading westward from New York. It needed workers to operate the new machines. A Mr. Young, foreman at Baer's, had shown off my skill, economy of motion, and economical use of material, to visiting buyers and "manufacturers." Mr. Young it was who was now engaged by the trust to start their Cleveland factory, and who, in turn, engaged me to learn the suction-machine method, and to teach it to other workers. Soon I was given charge of an entire floor, at fifteen dollars a week.

But my job lasted only a few weeks. A Mr. Weiss, vice-president of the newly-formed trust, was making a tour of inspection of their factories, and came to Cleveland. Early one morning the elderly superintendent of the building stopped me on my way up to the loft: "I'm sorry, Miss Pastor, but you can't go up to the suction-room." His words were like a blow. I could only stammer: "Why—why—what have I done?" "Mr. Weiss was here," said the superintendent. "He opened your desk, and found a book—" Yes, I understood. I had been reading a book, Vandervelde's *Collectivism*.[5] I went back to the bench where, by terrific driving, I earned between six and seven dollars a week. But the lesson in the antagonism between Capital and Labor sank deep.

One day, a young worker asked me why I don't join the Socialist Party. But how? I was eager. He explained the formality, and took me to a meeting. A crowd of men and women, young and old, stood about at the headquarters on Ontario Street. Here I was introduced to Max Hayes and Mrs. Hayes. They were newly-wed and seemed to have all eyes upon them. Mrs. nodded and Max Hayes, the most prominent Socialist leader in Cleveland, shook me by the hand and uttered a few perfunctory words of welcome. No one explained to me the nature of the party beyond saying "It was the party of the working class" and that it was "the duty of every working man and woman to vote for Socialism." A Red Card was issued to me and I attended a number of meetings. I wanted to learn more about socialism. But always I found a violent, wordy conflict in progress. Max Hayes and a white-haired man named Bandlow led the battle on one side. The other side was led by a wiry old worker who seemed to be asleep in his chair but proved quite wide awake when his turn came to take up the Billingsgate.

With nothing explained to me concerning the vital inner-party struggles, these violent discussions sounded senseless and offensive, and I drifted out. The few books that had been lent me, including the one over which I was "fired," were not for beginners. I got little out of them. I remained a "socialist by instinct." However, within the limited franchise for women I voted for socialist candidates (for school offices) when I became of voting age and went about with the vague notion that some day, in some way, we workers would abolish wage-slavery. When the local political boss, who had a saloon on Orange Street, asked me to "vote Democrat," I proudly announced that I was a socialist and would vote for socialist candidates only. Although friends had warned me that "without this man's good-will no good can come to anybody in the entire neighborhood."

Once a worker named Morris loaned me a copy of a magazine published in Chicago. I remember only one thing in it . . . The Factory Whistle, four lines. I never forgot them:

Across the flats, at dawn, the monster screams;
Its bulk blots the low sun. Ah, god of truth!
To wake from night's swift mockery of dreams,
To hear that hoarse throat clamoring for my youth!

The few radical workers near me did not enlighten me further. Once only was I drawn into their activities. An attempt was made to organize several of the stogie factories. We hired a little hall, got the workers to attend several times; speeches were made; the group held together. But when we applied for membership in the Cigar Makers Union, we were told by the American Federation of Labor that there was no room in the union for unskilled workers. The rebuff threw us back into our previous state of hopelessness, and the budding organization disbanded.

• • •

On Woodland Avenue, in a fine old house, working girls are being drawn into sewing classes, dancing classes, choruses, various other cultural activities. Miss Flora Mayer, "the kindest and best-loved school teacher in Cleveland" has started the Girls' Friendly Club, but before it is fairly developed, women of leisure living on Case, Cedar, and equally fine Avenues take the work into their own hands. Through Miss Mayer's visit to the factory I am drawn into the Club and avail myself of many of its activities. We working girls love Miss Mayer for her genuine love of us. And because she too works for a living. Some of us, at least, feel that she and the "ladies" belong to two different worlds.

Once the difference is sharply brought home to me. One of the "ladies" invited me and a shopmate to visit her home. I have never been inside of a rich man's home before. We are ushered into the drawing room . . . I step on a rug that must have cost hundreds of dollars! . . . I see costly pictures, vases; rich hangings, delicate, intricate, fabulous embroideries . . . I stare with astonishment at the furniture. One piece of it can cover the price of all the poor little heap of things we have struggled for years to pay for—out of our miserable wages, our endless labor! And they have all this, and no labor! . . . "What indifference to our lives to ask us here," I think, "to ask us to come and look upon it all!"

During the visit my words are few. Only my shopmate talks. It is dusk when we stroll homeward, past the fine houses on the Avenue. Behind the delicately-curtained, large clean windows, soft light glows through exquisite lamp shades. I know now what lies behind those windows I have seen.

"How would you like to live in one of those houses?" asked my shopmate.

"I want a decent world to live in, not a fine house."

"Don't those lights draw you?"

"I remember our slavery."

"But in there it's so sweet . . ."

"The essence of our bitter toil."

"But they're charming, cultured people."

"Out of our labor—all their leisure and their culture."

"Oh Rose, that's a terrible exaggeration."

"They don't work for a living, and when they occupy themselves, they do so to take what we make. No honest labor could give them all of this. There is no wealth without someone having worked for it. We, the workers, do the work, and create the wealth. We give them culture."

"If they find out at the Club that you're a Socialist . . ."

"What then?"

"They won't like it."

"I don't think to please them."

◆ ◆ ◆

Edwin Markham's "The Man With the Hoe," comes to the factory.[6] Worker hands it to worker. It goes from bench to bench. When it reaches me, I pounce upon it. "Let me have it for a day or two." "All right."

I rest the small volume of poetry open against my rack, roll a stogie and read as I roll; roll and read, read and roll, and by the end of the day commit the poem to memory. At the sink, where we gather to wash up, I recite it to the workers. I come home, and recite it to my mother and the children, to our neighbors, and explain, "So you see what the poet says—what will the rich do when this peasant, kept in darkness, in ignorance, working like a beast of burden, toiling without rest from dawn till dark, never asking why, never questioning—like a rock in his field, like a clod of earth turned by his hoe—what will they do when he rises, when he straightens that bent back of his and stands up, a Man, and shouts a Why that shakes the universe, that makes tremble all who have kept him in darkness and slavery? . . . A fine poet's question, eh, Neighbor?" . . . I was tussling with verse forms in the night hours, burying the brief essays under the mattress that no one might guess . . . But, as I read the poem and explained it, I was the peasant, not the poet: "*Of course, he will rise—we will rise—someday!*"

Morris Rosenfeld's "Songs of Labor" come to the shop.[7] I translate them at the bench. "Also a way of helping," I think to myself.

Flora Mayer is gone, married and gone to Indianapolis. The ladies of the Friendly Club are planning an evening's entertainment in the Club's new auditorium.

"Rose, will you contribute to the program?"

"I'll recite," I respond promptly.

So I was put on the program for "A Recitation."

The auditorium is crowded with members and leaders, and friends and relatives of both. Delightful skits and recitations are given by Miss Belle Goldsmith (soon to become Mrs. de Sola of Montreal and London) and several others. A Barn Dance, The Fiddler, De Crab-Apple and De Mudder-in-law, and similar light entertainment brought laughter and pleasant applause. My turn comes. I recite "The Man With the Hoe," and at the close hurled myself with such force into a chair that it broke. But as this was off stage, it caused no anti-climax.

It was always hard to keep my feet at rest when dance music played. But after the entertainment I was compelled to "sit out" the dances. The Club leaders cornered me and I was catechized about "The Man With the Hoe"! Where did I get it? When did I learn it? Didn't I know that the poem is about a French peasant? Didn't I know that for centuries the French peasantry has been kept in darkness and ignorance and poverty? Didn't I realize that here in America we had no such peasantry? That here the farmers are free and rich—at least, well-to-do and independent?

I told them what I know of workers' lives in America; what I had read of farming conditions. It is a relief to pour out to them the protest that had gathered in me to a point of physical pain. They seemed a bit appalled at my outburst.

After that, some of the club women visited me in my home. One sends new milk for the children from the cow that supplies her city table. Another brings me her outmoded coat for the winter. They kept an eye on us for a season. I was usually silent. But as they sat and chatted I was thinking: "We are being destroyed by poverty, by insecurity and overwork—we and our neighbors, we and our fellow workers, we and our class, and they come to apply a bit of court-plaster to the draining wound . . ."

◆ ◆ ◆

In the Friendly Club Chorus I learn many new songs, not songs of labor, but of birds and bees; of summer seas and little boats gleaming in the moonlight; of hills and stars and valleys; of forests, and of bees and birds again. Nature poems—pleasant songs for working girls! Upon me these songs do not have the desired effect. Instead of being content with singing about those things, I yearn to be close to them. Is rest and recreation only for the rich and the idle? Why cannot I who work so hard, who give many thousands of people the "delight of a good smoke" many thousand times over—why cannot I go into the hills, on the waters, into the woods? Is rest and recreation never to be mine? Twice I had attempted to take a week-end vacation, and on both occasions nearly met with disaster. At a suburban farm where a young friend lived with her old parents I was given canned food that had nearly poisoned me. Later, another week-end at a similar farm got me a crushed ankle that kept me on crutches for fourteen weeks, with no chance to stop work for any part of the time. "The poor," I had laughed wryly, "had no right even to a week-end rest." Once or twice I had been to a city park, where boats could be hired and rowing afforded for an hour. At another time I ventured a long way from home, on a big boat. Weary, heavy-limbed workers and harried, worried mothers with many children were packed upon its decks that Sunday. The boat was bound for a public beach. I had the baby in my arms, two of the children clinging close to my skirts, who in turn held the hands of the other two tots. All our five children. On the Monday I was a leaden-handed worker, and paid dearly for my holiday.

A holiday—a *real* holiday! Why should we have all the labor, all the sweating in the cities where, on the hot days, we leave the work bench every fifteen minutes to run cold water from the tap over our wrists, in order not to go mad with the heat? Why should others who do not work so hard, or who do not work at all, have all the cool breezes, the ocean, the hills and dales, the peace, the silence, the solitude, the cool for which our entire beings seek in vain, as we turn from the tap to sweat at the bench again, till we can bear no more and rush again to the tap? . . . Who designed it all? Who says that it must always be like this? . . .

And so the nature songs taught at the club to bring contentment to those who had deep cause for discontent intensified my rebelliousness. I keep dreaming of the day when I might "hit that thing"—our slavery. I dance, I sing; at rare times, there is a wedding, a dance, and a party; I read poetry and the classics. But under it all I am up in arms against that which holds us in poverty and insecurity, and ever-burdened us with labor. And when I have a vote to cast I cast it for the Socialist Party candidates with the feeling that I am performing a sacred function! . . .

● ● ●

A woman with a very beautiful voice comes to the Friendly Club. She sings for us and hears us in chorus. She selected me for solo work, and pronounced my voice a "mezzo-soprano of rare range and quality," and insisted that it be trained.

The gift of song is precious to me. When I bring scraps of melody to the shop—snatches just learned, or the whole of some song sweet as the memory of my uncle's garden, brief as my childhood, my fellow workers listen, intent; in their eyes wonder, or tears. Knives beat on rolling boards; hands clap; cutters rattle; calls come to "sing it again." And I, glad that they too love the song; that they, on hearing it, are as moved as I was when I first heard it. I feel grateful for the ability to re-create the magic for them. "Some day," I dream, "I shall move thousands . . ."

After the singer hears me and praises my voice, she gives me my first lesson in her studio. I declare I will study at whatever sacrifice. Not to pauperize me, Alma Wolf charges me only fifty cents a lesson. It is so little. But after two lessons I am compelled to remember that fifty cents buys ten loaves of bread. I go to the studio no more. The dream gnaws at me and will not let me rest. But I cannot escape reality. Often, as I struggle with myself over the question of that fee, I watched my mother and the children, eating their meager meal, thinking: "I'm as hungry to learn as they to eat. Oh, if I could sing—sing for the world!" And tears of frustration fill my eyes till the children seemed a blur and the bread they ate unreal.

But even as I love song I love the faces of my comrades in the factory, of my mother and father, the children, our neighbors; of working people in the streets, in other public places. Of the light behind these faces I drink and never have enough. Once, years afterward, I saw a dog rescued from a rock in the Long Island Sound to which he must have scrambled in his fight for life when those who wanted to be rid of him had thrown him into the water from a boat, or pier, or high bluff—who knows? He was almost a skeleton when found, and so exhausted he could stand on his helpless legs only by swinging from side to side—like a disturbed pendulum. How long he had struggled there before he reached the rock, how long he had been on the rock before help came, none could guess. But when water was set before him, he drank as though for the rest of his life he wanted nothing but water; or, as though, doomed to die within the hour, he was bent upon packing into that hour a lifetime's joy of drinking water. He drank until it seemed he must die of the preposterous excess! And still he lapped and lapped with uninterrupted concentration, with terrifying eagerness . . .

So I drink of the light in human faces. Infinite shades, infinite nuances: Faces whose loveliness is almost too great to be borne; plain faces whose sweetness makes the heart leap with wonder; faces that set the heart singing or fill the heart with an alien grief that becomes its own; faces like weariness that follows the toiling day. Sometimes, there are ugly faces; or faces that hurt—like the ones that cruel environment had stamped upon some human countenances. And oh, the beautiful, defiant faces of my few comrades! Even Sophie's face—homely, pock-marked Sophie, who sits near me at the shop. An insupportable sweetness lurks in the corners of Sophie's mouth. My joy proves more than an aesthetic joy to me. It makes me more completely one with my world, until "compensation" for my lack of opportunity to develop my gift of song is no longer needed. "I will sing here, among my own; in the factory, in my home to my neighbors. It is enough to see the light in their faces . . ." With this thought I often go to sleep at night, content; or awake in the dawn at the call of our terrible chanticleer, eager for the shop.

♦ ♦ ♦

Once, someone brings a copy of a new publication to the factory—MacFadden's *Physical Culture Magazine*. I pounce upon it. A healthy body, "the body beautiful"! A fine ideal. But how many workers can attain it? "Still it's worth striving for," I say to myself: open windows at night; no tea; no coffee; no corsets (I had never worn them though the universal ideal was an 18-inch waistline); no late hours. But to what end? To the end that I shall bring a healthy body and mind to the cause of the workers. When? How? I do not know. Some day—somehow. I must be prepared. Now, when there is food enough, it must be the right kind of food. Now when there is enough to buy a garment, I must make it a sensible garment. My shoes must have a sensible heel, my shoulders must be thrown back when I walk—even though at work I am compelled to lean over and crowd my lungs. What bodily good I can wrest from my wretched environment, that I must wrest; to this end—to this one end. . . .

♦ ♦ ♦

When the burden of the struggle for bread became more than he could bear, my step-father left home.

The first time he went away—without warning, my mother and I stayed awake all night. What could it mean? A mishap? The River? We invented a hundred causes, but fell silent with the approach of dawn. The day's work would soon begin. In the grey light my mother went from child to sleeping child, gazing upon it and wringing her hands.

I kissed her before I left for the shop:

"Don't worry, Mamele, I'll work harder than ever, you'll see. I will never leave you."

Her tears were still on my cheek when I boarded the street car.

Dreary days passed with no word from him. At first we thought to inquire at Police Headquarters; then decided, better not. "Better not to know ever," said my mother, "than to place our troubles on record with the police."

We scanned the columns of the newspapers, hoping, fearing to find his name. Months. No word, no clue. I worked impossible hours now at a frantic pace. But at least there was an air of peace at home. My mother was more silent, but less often in tears. The children lost weight, but for a spell they were not tormented.

One evening I came from work to find him seated by the kitchen stove.

"Hullo, Rosalie."

"Hello, father."

Simply, quietly. As if he had not been gone for months without leaving any trace.

"How are you, Rosalie?"

"I'm all right, father."

And life took up the broken thread—and continued to weave the familiar pattern into the fabric of our nights and days.

Once I found him, after a long absence, sitting close to the stove in the very chair in the very attitude in which I had seen him last: slightly bent forward, clay pipe in mouth, an elbow on knee, hand on the pipe. (In 1931, while under X-ray treatment by Professor Hans Holfelder[8] at the Roentgen Institute, Frankfurt, I attended an exhibition of modern art. On entering one of the galleries I was startled by a life size painting of my step-father, so completely he, that I caught my breath in a rush of painful memories. The canvas proved to be Cezanne's famous "The Carter.") I had just come in from a rare holiday spent in a city park with Bess, my shopmate and friend. The day in the sun with water and boat and a pair of oars had raised my spirits. I threw open the door and entered with a burst of song and laughter. But when I saw my father seated quietly by the stove, a sudden hush fell upon me. I stood dumb, ashamed to have been glad before him. What was it—what was it in his face? . . . A great sorrow for the man seized me. He had suffered; more than I, the young girl could suffer. So long away! And now so quietly seated in the kitchen corner—furrows deep in his forehead, and running deeper over the drawn cheeks . . .

"Hello, Father," gently, contritely.

"Hullo, Rosalie," he responded.

"Supper is ready," my mother announced quietly.

We drew up our chairs, and ate our supper. Between long silences were words of one syllable—like a few dark beads on a long white string.

• • •

Now we are living on Woodland Avenue. Many of our neighbors are Negroes. We feel at one with them. They too are poor, hard-working, oppressed. We feel we belong together. Our children play with their children. Our door is always open to them—their doors, to us. Once I hear a white neighbor's child call a little black boy a name in prejudice against his color. I cry out. The white child runs and I run too, catch up with her, hold her, and make her see that workers' children, black and white, belong together. . . .

Woodland Avenue. That too is where Simon comes. Simon! Soft, dark eyes; hair blue-black; pale cheeks; wide generous mouth; red lips. A romantic-looking young man! And a "thirty-second cousin." His family moved from Pittsburgh to Cleveland—and here he is! "Simon is a fine young man," my mother notes for my benefit, and I agree with a blush— a rosy shroud instantaneously woven for the old love that died on the instant. . . .

Simon works in the needle trades, and he has an ideal of his own. "When we are married," he asserts one Saturday afternoon, "I'll open a tailor-shop and make money. I'll buy you a watch and chain and a necklace of pearls, and you'll wear silk dresses."

"No," I retort, hotly, "I'm a Socialist, and don't want jewels and fine clothes. I want to be like any other worker."

"When you're my wife," says Simon proudly and emphatically, "you'll wear silks and jewels, I say."

"I won't!" and I too am emphatic.

Over this we quarrel several times. But the quarrels are needless. One day, at a picnic, Simon became infatuated with another girl. I hear of it and with my friend, Bessie, I hurry to his mother's house. There I find Simon seated at the kitchen table, eating his supper. Without a word I take off the ring he has given me and lay it on the table near him. Whereupon he faints dead away! His mother shrieks, "You are killing my son! It is you and not her he wants to marry." "He doesn't care for me, and I won't have him like that," I tell her, though I don't know where I got the courage to break with Simon. The ring which she has forced back into my hand, I fling back at her unconscious son, and leave the house before he has time to revive.

Simon married soon thereafter. Not the girl of the picnic, but another. He also acquired the sweatshop of his dreams.

The wolf that is said to be in a growing boy's stomach is also in a young girl's heart. The days were like great gaping mouths that never shut content. But chance was to provide me with another distant devotion . . .

We were living at 766 Sterling Avenue when a neighbor brought my mother home copies of the *Jewish Daily News*. The editor of its English page was calling for suggestions from his readers. IF YOU ARE IN BUSINESS, WRITE A LETTER! DO YOU WORK IN AN OFFICE? WRITE A LETTER! DO YOU WORK IN THE FACTORY? WRITE A LETTER! In arresting type at the ends of columns, between articles, between short items the invitation went forth in bold-faced type to all and sundry: WRITE A LETTER! WRITE A LETTER! WRITE A LETTER! I would never have written that letter had it not been for Mark Twain. His "Punch, Brothers, punch for fare, punch in the presence of the passenger" was brought to the factory by some wag of a fellow worker. The entire shop took to sing-songing it and the doggerel made me hear my alarm clock, early and late, tick words instead of moments:

"Do-you-work-in-the-factory? Write-a-letter. Do-you-work-in-the-fac-to-ry? Write-a-let-ter."

The call was constant and this nonsense amused me. Finally, July 16, 1901, I responded to the chatter of my 98-cent clock, and wrote a bantering letter—wrote it in the factory during the lunch hour, addressed it to the editor, and posted it in the spirit of a lark.[9] After some days the effusion appeared in the English department and I received a long missive in the editor's own hand urging me to tell him more of myself, of the shop, of my life at home. I wrote again and he replied—inviting me, this time to contribute; preferably talks to the girls. The invitation pleased and excited me. Was I not "confidential advisor" to dozens of my shopmates? Ready for the "call," I acted without delay, and wrote my first talk that night, beginning after eleven o'clock, and posting the manuscript at four in the morning. With a pang I dropped it into the box. "What if the editor should change his mind and return it?" I could not sleep the two hours left to me of the night for thinking of the possible disappointment. But the article was accepted and I received a two-dollar check for my labor.

So I became a columnist of the English Department of the *Jewish Daily News* and burnt the candle at both ends. Frequently, I would write much more than a column; at times, two; but no matter what the length, there was always the two dollars—big as cartwheels in the eyes of my Need. And my mother would protest, "But Rosalie, you can't keep this up. It will ruin your health."

Until the winter of 1902—about a year and a half, all told—I continued writing and sending the "talks" with regularity, although I had to use the better part of my nights for the work. Meanwhile, letters to and from the editor became more frequent and intimate. Once he took a long journey just to see me. After that meeting our friendship-by-correspondence took on new color. There were declarations . . . and again there were dreams . . . Yes—we shall be married and live happily ever afterward . . . We shall be married, and I shall not be compelled to wear a gold watch and chain, a pearl necklace and silk dresses! We shall be married and together work for the people. . . .

"Either the writing or the work in the factory must go," said my mother, coming to me, day after day, with the same cry, "You can't do both; you'll break down; and what will we do then?"

. . . I could understand my mother's anxiety. I was then the only support of the family—eight of us. My father had gone from home. We had long since given up all hope of seeing or hearing from him again. He never came back. We never saw him again. Several evenings a week I worked in a "buckeye," the rest of my evenings I devoted to teaching English to adult immigrants in the Jewish Educational Alliance Building, where our Friendly Club was housed. Strain as I might from eleven to twelve hours daily, I could not earn more than five or six dollars a week in the factory. My pace was broken. My pace would never come back. The only hours in which I could earn the two extra dollars at writing were those torn from sleep. My pace was broken and my mother feared that I too would break. The question had to be settled: "Shall I earn an uncertain extra two dollars and risk my health, or drop writing and stay at the bench for a more or less certain five or six dollars?" Of course I dropped the writing. We were eight human beings living on five or six dollars a week. Some will ask: "How is it possible?" The answer is: "sickness, semi-starvation, despair." These will only be words to some. But I *know*. Every wage-worker *knows*. I have not forgotten. Were I to live fifty times fifty years I could not forget all that these words imply. But I cannot tell their meaning here. I cannot write it and be believed— save by those of us who know; and for us it is enough to say: sickness, semi-starvation, despair . . .

♦ ♦ ♦

It is early one frosty morning during that winter. A homeless man knocks at our kitchen door. My mother opens it.

"For the love of God, give me something to eat," says the man.

My mother looks at the man, looks at me, at the children, and again at the man. . . . "Poor gentile!" . . . What can we do? Turn him away?

We invite him in. I brew a little black coffee (chicory, really)—all there is.

There is half a loaf of bread for the children; no more food of any kind, not even sugar to sweeten the coffee.

I bring the black coffee in a big cup to the table and place it before the hungry man. My mother cuts the bread into slices.

"Eat, eat," says my mother.

The hungry man eats every morsel of bread and drinks up the coffee, while my mother stands humbly before him apologizing for having no sugar in the house. . . .

When he is gone we chuckle together, close to tears. Out of her ancient training my mother had moaned before the knock came—"If God would only send us relief!"

"So you see what God sent us," I laugh and cry. "The rich would say that God both made and sent him and that God will feed him."

"Yes, yes," my mother shook her head and mused. "But who will feed the poor if not the poor?"

"No one, Mamele, no one. But God didn't make the poor, and no God will unmake poverty. Only—we!"

CHAPTER III

Journalism and Marriage

The early winter months passed and I continued to send no "copy" to New York. The editor wrote and wrote again, insistent. Why, why don't I write? Finally, I confessed and drew the picture for him of our situation and our struggles. Meanwhile, in the office of the *Jewish Daily News* hundreds of letters were being received from all parts of the country: "What has become of Zelda?" (My pen name.) It worried the publisher; until, finally he decided to offer me a permanent position on the paper. One day I rushed to my mother with two letters received in the same mail. One contained the offer from the publisher; the other was the last of several hundred letters from A.H.F. (A.H. Fromenson)—editor of the English Department. It began with "Ho for New York!" and described to me how he had taken advantage of "the right moment" to impress the publisher with the necessity of asking me to become assistant to himself. . . .

My mother embraced me, and danced about the kitchen for very joy; while I assured her over and over that I would soon bring her to New York together with the children. Several were with us at the time, while the others had been placed in a "home." "Charity" was trying to save us from annihilation when the publisher's note came—with its offer of fifteen dollars a week.

Thus, by virtue of a suggestion by Mark Twain, I left Cleveland—

after twelve years in the cigar factories—to take up life and work in the City of New York.

◆ ◆ ◆

At the Pennsylvania Railway Station (then on the New Jersey side), I arrived, expectant. A.H.F. was not there to meet the train as he had offered. I crossed on the ferry to New York. "No one will be at the other end," I said to myself. He was not there. I sat down to wait but soon remembered that I knew no one in this million-folked city. "What if I am late? Where will I go for the night?" I leaped up from the bench and stopped a passing guard, who directed me to a funny little horse-car. This I boarded, though I might have walked, the time it took to snail across to 185 East Broadway.

All I possessed was in a small telescope bag. I gripped this bag as I went up the stoop to the business office of the *Jewish Daily News* and asked for the editor of the English Department. A young man with thick glasses left the office, walked down the hall a bit and pointed out the door. I entered a sordid little back room where A.H.F. himself was slamming down the cover of his roll-top desk. His stenographer was putting on her hat. "Mr. Fromensen?" I inquired. (He had cautioned me to be formal.) "Miss Pastor? . . . Let me introduce you to Belle Shapiro. . . ." And Belle invited me to stay with her till I get my bearings. "Report at nine tomorrow morning, please," the editor said and was gone.

◆ ◆ ◆

Evening: Mrs. Shapiro is cooking supper, standing before the kitchen range.

Belle, and her younger sister Bess, and I are also in the kitchen.

Mrs. Shapiro is kind, motherly. She hails from Suwalk, not many miles from Augustova, where I was born. Already I feel like one of the family. Indeed, she catechizes me as though I were one of her daughters and takes me to her heart. Her questions come naturally, and already I answer them as though it were a matter of course: Family, children, wages, friends, all personal questions. Simple, direct. I answer them directly and simply. Then she comes to the subject of A.H.F.:

"How long have you known him?"

"For nearly two years—by correspondence."

"Never saw him before?"

"Once. He came to see me. We talked for two hours or more between trains."

"Has he ever written you about other women?"

"Why—yes. I think he told me everything."

"Did he ever tell you about a Miss ———?"

"No. Who is she?"

"The woman he is going to marry, some day."

I am silent.

"You are not interested?"

"Yes—yes, of course."

I hear the story of an eight-years' engagement. . . .

"He—he is still engaged to her?"

"Still. And everybody knows it—everybody, but you."

"Oh."

January 23, 1903. I am installed at a desk in the little back room, and the process of breaking me in begins. I must associate much with the editor, but I decide to associate little with the man.

Some dreams, however, take time to dispel. I have a long struggle with myself. Perhaps this conflict had as much to do with my getting "licked into shape" as had the editor's daily hammering.

Be that as it may, I felt that both were good for me. I worked at all hours and got practical newspaper and editorial training. A.H.F., and I as his assistant, had to find all the material that went into the English section—now changed from a weekly to a daily page. As "Zelda" I wrote "Just Between Ourselves Girls"; I also became "The Observer" and wrote sketches and impressions of the East Side; I made contributions in prose and verse under my own name. From time to time I published original aphorisms under the caption "Ethics of the Dustpan." I read exchanges and clipped suitable material. On rare occasions, when the editor was absent, I wrote the English editorials. Not being politically awake I was unaware of being guided. I took every suggestion gratefully and in good faith. Reading back, I find my material dominated by the traditional viewpoint, with here and there a radical deviation.[1] Such deviations usually slipped through into the columns of the *Jewish Daily News* only because of carelessness on the part of the responsible editors. For example, there were the lines:

> The wealth by rich men reached and kept
> Was not obtained by fingers ten;
> Ah no! For while the rich men slept
> The wealth-producers worked for them.

These lines contain more of truth than poetry; indeed more of truth than the publisher would have knowingly let slip by. In the main, however, I concerned myself with personal relationships; problems of the home. Rarely was there a flash of the social viewpoint.

The paper is a devil-fish. I feel its tentacles about me, no time to read, no time to think, no more books. I am sucked up into a maw hungrier than that of the factory. No free hours. All hours are for the paper. All thought in my so-called free time is to be utilized for the columns.

At night I am sandwiched in between Bess and Belle. The bed is barely wide enough for two. Bess and Belle are both air-shy. I suffocate in the little room with its one window open just a crack. The Shapiros, their two daughters, several small children and I, are in the tiny five room flat on Madison Street. Hot summer evenings we drag mattresses to the roof. Even on the roof the nights are gasping. I move to another flat in the neighborhood, stay one night and return. Mrs. Shapiro is like a mother to me. She watches over me jealously. Here I feel safe.

I walk against the endless stream, peering into every face . . . I lean out of the window, and watch the tenement life about me . . . Mothers on stoops or on fire-escapes, babies at breast, struggling for air as Mrs. Feinberg struggled when she was dying. "Little mothers"—children of eight or nine, lugging infants too heavy for their slight bodies. Little children on the streets at midnight—racing, dashing, "playing"—who must fall exhausted before they can sleep in the stifling tenement holes they call "home" . . . "Oh God, Oh God, Oh God." The old cry takes me. And then comes the electrifying thought: "And there need not be poverty any more!"

Someone suggests ice-cream . . . I dare not spend the nickel. Bed and board I must have. But the rest is for my mother and the children.

The editor asks me to walk out with him one evening. I decline. Best not to go. . . .

Daily, at the noon hour, Belle and I mount the four flights of stairs to her mother's flat, take a hurried dinner, and return to the office.

A few times I venture to the Metropolitan Museum. Always I promise myself to go often, but am too spent when the rest days come to take the trip so far uptown.

◆ ◆ ◆

In time I get acquainted with the force at 185 East Broadway. The men on the editorial staff, the men in the composing room—where I spend some time daily to make-up the page. I like them all, and like Zevin best; Zevin, the deformed one—breastbone and backbone "hunched." He is the kindest of them all, chuck-full of humor—known as "Tashrak" the Feiulletonist, the creator of thousands of side-splitting tales. He likes me, too, and befriends me. Besides, he sees a bit of "Socialism," and we talk. During an election period I observe strange comings and goings. Men closet themselves with the publishers in a small conference room. They come out flushed; glad, and excited. I ask Zevin what it is all about. He explains: "Newspapers are all like that. Corrupt. Take money from both capitalist parties—sell their columns outright." During the campaign I am approached with a suggestion—if I would write . . . I "fly off the handle" . . . Apologies. Really, nothing was intended . . . What rottenness! Zevin agrees. "But they all do it—all. Advertisers, money, control the press and through the press control politics—everything."

Candidates for office come to the editorial rooms, rabbis, presidents of societies, every manner of East Side worthy. They all want something. "Publicity," they call it. I chuckle to hear the word. It is a funny word I have never heard before. A swarthy, wiry little man comes in. He has the face of a gypsy and a great shock of wiry black hair. He too is looking for "publicity." "A favorable story about my song," he demands. He is evidently without money, but the staff likes him. The editors, the re-write men are pleased to see him and say friendly things. They slap him on the back. He glimpses me. "Hello, who is this red-head?" He comes and puts his face up close to mine. I recoil. He is half drunk and smelling of garlic. "Shame upon you! Get away!" He is repulsive and insolent.

He declaims: "I drink—and I eat garlic . . . If the woman will not let me kiss her, I know she does not love me. I test her love . . . You don't know me? I'm a fortunate man . . . What, you don't know who I am? I'm Imber! Imber the poet! the poet of the Zionists, the writer of their song—" 'The Hatikve.' " [2]

At times, he comes in quite drunk. My heart aches for the wretched man, another Edgar Allen Poe—a genius burning himself up in poverty and despair. Late one evening I find him lying in a heap under a lamp-post on Grand Street. Children are tormenting him, kicking him about, plucking at his clothing, at his long, wiry, curling and matted mass of black hair. I get him to his feet and scatter the children. "Now come!" I say, trying to guide his steps. But he will not walk with me. "All right, you walk alone, and go directly to the *Tageblatt* office." He can barely lurch along, he is so drunk. A few of the children follow and jeer. I compel him to move on. Every dozen paces he turns to curse me, but keeps going. Someone is in the office, and he is allowed to spend the night there. How fortunate!

In the morning he is respectful and sober. "She brought me in," he declares with a grand bow as I enter the editorial room. "The Rose of Compassion"—"I must write a poem to her." "You are a poet—a singer. Stop drinking, Imber. A poet! and you brutalize yourself. . . ." At the same moment I remember my socialist instruction; the individual is a victim of social forces beyond his control. . . .

He died not long after; died of alcoholism—of poverty and wretchedness. The poor Zionists could not help him, and the rich Zionists had other things to occupy them. . . .

I meet other poets, writers in the old tradition. Eliakum Zunser.[3] I am thrilled to see the old singer in the flesh. I've sung his songs of immigrant life—to my shopmates, to my neighbors, sitting on stoops, in yards, on warm nights, by kitchen stoves on winter evenings.

There was also the young generation of Zunsers, and young Shomers too, children of the old novelist.[4] Somewhat radical they were then. We would meet and talk. Young Annie Shomer had studied singing. She possessed a fine voice. I would sit and listen to her. She too loved the folk songs. "Someday she will move thousands," I would think and sigh for my lost opportunity.

Of such was my new life in New York.

◆ ◆ ◆

Of the constant stream of people who come and go at the editorial rooms, a tall stranger stops at my desk one afternoon; stops, and wants to say something, but finds it hard to speak.

"I . . . I'm a countryman of yours," he stammers at last. "Perhaps you would like to know where . . . Jacob the Shoemaker is."

"Jacob the— You know where he is—where I can see him?"

"Yes, I know. He is the same proud, lonely man—and still at the bench though now he cobbles shoes; he does not make them," said the stranger. "He doesn't know you are here but maybe you'd like to see him . . . I knew Sam, too."

"Sam? Sam visited us in Cleveland once. Where is he now?"

"I don't know," said the stranger. "Plying the same old needle wherever he is, I suppose."

I can hardly wait till evening. After supper I walk the short distance east on Madison Street till I find a sign that reads "Scammel Street." What a poor little pocket of a place! Narrow; old houses; funny little shops. On my right, near the end of the street, in a tiny shop window I see old shoes piled. This is the place. In a very coffin of a store—so narrow is it—a slight little man with greying hair sits bent over a shoe, mending it. The face I do not see. Nor does he see the face outside the narrow shop window.

I pass through the open door into the cobbler's shop, and stand before the cobbler.

"Good evening," I say.

"Good evening," he answers, and looks up from the shoe he is mending.

"Are you busy?"

"You see . . . I must finish this."

"Only a heel to mend," I plead, and my heart is pounding. So white the face! And the eyes nearly blinded. Pity fills me. Maybe I can help . . . There must be ways . . .

"Well—if it's only a heel . . ."

I take off my shoe and hold it out to him. Our hands touch for the space of a breath as he takes the shoe from me . . . He works on it . . . I am silent. Later—

"I have greetings for you," I venture.

"You have? From whom?" His eyes are raised for a moment, puzzled.

"Your son."

"My son?" He is eager. His face, his all but blinded eyes, kindled. "You know Sam?" He smiles, a smile turned inward—addressed to memories of Samuel.

"Yes. I met him—In Cleveland . . . There I met your . . . daughter, too."

"My daughter! I have no daughter!" He flings it back sharply. His face grew hard. Then softened again. "But tell me about Sam. How was he? Was he well? Did he have work? . . . Did you like my son? . . . I've lost track of my son . . . Eh," he sighed . . . "There, I think the heel is all right now."

"How much?"

"Only fifteen cents . . . Thank you . . . Come again."

The following week, the tall stranger again stood before my desk.

"Jacob has left New York," said the tall stranger.

"Left New York! Why, what for?"

"He was afraid you might prove to be Hindl's daughter and make demands upon him."

"I . . . Why, I would have tried to help! I . . ."

"Well—he was afraid. So he sold his gold watch and chain, and his cobbler's shop and went off to Denver . . ."

I never saw Jacob the Learned Bootmaker again. Several years later I heard that he had died "somewhere in the west."

• • •

At the Jewish Educational Alliance two groups of girls met. One from a club at the University Settlement; the other from a club at the Alliance. They formed one club and sent a request to me to come and be their leader for the summer months. Their own leaders had gone to the country. The heat was suffocating, the work in the office taxing. Besides, I was deep in the task of preparing a flat for my mother and the children. So I declined the invitation. But the girls were stubborn and I finally yielded. We met once a week in a room at the Alliance Building, which was a few doors from the *Daily News* office. We talked, read books and papers, and discussed individual and home problems. At times, I spoke to them about Socialism and passed on the few vague concepts which were then mine on the subject. These talks stirred and interested the girls, and I was glad. But soon the meeting place in the Alliance was denied us, for some reason; so we gathered in the three-room flat on lower Grand Street to which my mother and several of the children had come. There, on chairs and boxes, tables and floors and beds, we'd sit and hold earnest discussion. At the summer's end their club leaders returned and since the understanding had been that I would stay only until the return of their leaders, I refused to be an interloper and promptly left the girls to the old leadership. But they refused to accept the change. They would waylay me as I came from the office and hammer away at my resistance. Sonya Levien—one of the girls—Sonya of the blue eyes and black hair, and the smile as kind as my grandfather's cried real tears as we stood on the curb debating the matter. I finally relented and offered a compromise; I would *visit* the club provided the leader raised no objection.

"And where will I find you," I asked.

"At the University Settlement," they said.

◆ ◆ ◆

The University Settlement? . . . I had interviewed a Mr. J.G. Phelps Stokes there, in July. . . .[5]

During June and July of that year (1903) Mr. Fromensen decided to break me in as an interviewer, and I didn't like the process. I felt that the office was seeking to "direct the tone" of the interviews. This irritated me and I had quarreled with the editor. He threatened to dismiss me. "You'll go back to the cigar factory, young woman, unless you do as you're told." "Who controls my job, controls my life!" My thoughts were bitter but I dared not throw up my job. By and bye, however, I was more at ease. They seemed to have given up the interviewing idea. But the matter again came up. One Friday morning Fromensen said: "Miss Pastor, Mr. J.G. Phelps Stokes, millionaire resident of the University Settlement is reported to have resigned from the council and to be planning a rival settlement. We want to know all about it, and I have arranged for an interview for eight-thirty this evening. Go and get the story." So there were still to be interviewing assignments! I flew into a passion, and so too did he. He stamped up and down the room and so too did I. He insisted; I pleaded. He was obdurate. "You get that interview this evening, young lady, or don't come back on Monday morning." There was no help for me. . . .

After supper at the Madison Street flat I wandered about Seward Park inwardly turbulent. I could not leave the job—yet. I could not bring myself to turn northward toward the corner of Eldridge and Rivington streets, where stood the University Settlement. Indeed, I do not know what the outcome would have been had I not run into the genial little Edward King.[6] Edward King, the popular little old Scotchman of the East Side, was due to deliver a lecture on some libertarian subject at the Educational Alliance. But I button-holed him and would not let him go. He must come along to do the talking for me. But how could he? His audience was waiting. Preposterous! Impossible! I hung on. "You must come, you must. I could never talk to the old fogie myself." (I had visions of a stern old man with a long grey beard sitting on a throne, a sort of rich man's Jehova.) "But my dear Miss Pastor, I. . . ." He struggled. Useless! In sight of the building, in view of the lights where his audience waited, he was compelled to turn his back on the lecture hall and walk northward with me . . .

I wrote the interview in the Madison Street flat that night. But it was really old Edward King who got J.G. Phelps Stokes to talk, while I listened—listened and looked—enchanted by the very tall slender young man who both in features and in general appearance was so like the young Abe Lincoln, and so full of sympathy for the poor. . . .

As Edward King and I were leaving the apartment the tall young "Lincoln" looked down upon me benignly from his height of six feet four inches (Lincoln's height, too!) to say good night, "and I should like to read the interview before it is published," he said. So I mailed him my copy early that (Saturday) morning, and on Monday he brought it to the office in person. I was out for an early lunch and missed the unexpected call. "Eh, you red-head, Mr. Stokes brought this back himself, and said it was punk," teased Fromensen. My face fell. "Aw, cheer up, it's not so bad. He liked it; and was disappointed not to see you again—actually said he was sorry you were out. So there!" And shortly thereafter a report was current to the effect that Mr. Stokes had left the University Settlement. . . .

So, when I visited the girls one Saturday afternoon in November and was afterward piloted from the club-room to the top floor and the "tea" in the residents' quarters, I was happily surprised to look up from my preferred cup of hot water into the large, earnest grey eyes of a very tall slender young man with the face of an Abe Lincoln. He looked benignly down upon me and seemed glad to see me . . . and he had not gone from the University Settlement, after all!

Before I left the residents' quarters Mr. Stokes had invited me—

together with several other young women (among them Margaret Wein, an unusually beautiful woman who later became the wife of Marcel Cachin, the noted French Communist Deputy), to take Thanksgiving dinner with him at the Settlement.[7]

◆ ◆ ◆

That winter and the following spring found me a frequently-invited guest of Mr. Stokes. In the dining room of the building, at its long refectory table, were always between thirty and forty residents and their guests. Conversation covered the widest possible range of topics discussed from widely varying points of view. Seated somewhere not far from Mr. Stokes at the head of the table, I would listen, but rarely speak. What was there that I could say to all those learned gentlemen and brilliant ladies—to professors, publicists, doctors, lawyers, scientists, educators, scholars! Perhaps, had I been compelled to talk, I would have stood up and said "Ladies and gentlemen . . . and there need not be poverty any more. . . ." And perhaps this would have shocked the fine company. Worse still, I would have been unable to give any learned reason for the faith that was in me . . . But when I went down several flights of stairs to the girls' clubs I talked freely, even eloquently. They were like me. Their homes were like my home, their parents like mine. We spoke a common tongue, the language of the struggling poor. They understood me, and glowed with enthusiasm as I with eloquence. I always felt that I had a message for them, that to them I had something to say.

But I was constantly being drawn into new circles, making new contacts continually. Margaret Wein—"Lilete" her friends called her—organized a group for the study of Ward's *Pure Sociology*. Mr. Stokes was invited to join. Through his influence the invitation was extended to me. Several years afterward, I read the book with much profit but at the time the work was like a foreign language to me. Nevertheless, I attended and struggled to grasp something of its lessons. In the group I met Algernon Lee, one of the leaders of the Socialists and Leonard D. Abbott, libertarian, and others with whom I later worked. Many notable people came to the settlement. Madame Breshkovskaya, "Babushka," little grandmother of the Russian Revolution, was among them.[8] Thirteen years later she was to prove unequal to the Proletarian Revolution. But I remember how profoundly she impressed me at the time. She learned English in a Russian prison. She was going back to Russia to help the Revolution. Perhaps she would be captured, perhaps die in prison. It did not matter to her. She would be serving the cause of "the people." How was I to know that to her "the people" were not the proletariat? So Russia's revolution had one of its iron leaders in this gentle white-haired woman, member of the Russian aristocracy. How impressed I was.

Emma Goldman—who in later years was to inveigh against the necessary Proletarian Dictatorship, but was to spend her remaining years at peace with the Dictatorship of the Bourgeoisie—Emma Goldman, too, was a guest at the Settlement in those days. William English Walling was prominent among the resident workers, as was Ernest Poole, and Leroy Scott. Both resident workers and guests were full of fine enthusiasms on the subject of the struggling poor . . . Few of these were to survive the acid test of the Russian Proletarian Revolution. But in those days they were the sources of my inspiration. Anarchists, Single-taxers, Socialists, Social reformers of various schools—both visitors and resident workers . . . The University Settlement was a seething center for the exchange of ideas; and contact with these schools of thought and these glowing advocates stirred more deeply in me the old desire to serve my class—the countless millions who toil and live in poverty and wretchedness and insecurity.

◆ ◆ ◆

Among the visitors at the settlement were the Barrows, old friends of Mr. Stokes.[9] They were Mr. and Mrs. Samuel Barrows and their daughter Mabel, who was presenting Greek plays given in the ancient Greek, herself acting in them. The Barrows had invited Mr. Stokes to Cedar Lodge—their summer camp on Lake Memphramagog in the province of Quebec, and the invitation was extended to include me. I was pleased, but also at a loss as to what to do with it. Mr. Stokes urged me to accept, and added that Miss Louise Lockwood (a mutual friend from the College Settlement) was also going.

The invitation was for the first two weeks in August, and it was then early Spring. Time enough to save up the railroad fare! But I debated the question with my mother. Would it not place a special burden on us? "Accept," urged my mother, "if Mr. Stokes wants so much to have you go." He had "seen" me home from the Settlement on many occasions, and my mother liked him. "Always so kind, and thoughtful, and polite." And Zevin my devoted friend, when he heard of the invitation, though he looked sad, urged me to accept and offered to lend me the money for the railroad tickets.

So it was decided in the spring that in August I would go with Mr. Stokes and Miss Lockwood.

Meanwhile, during June and July, Mr. Stokes called at my home not infrequently. We had moved to Webster Avenue, in the Bronx, to be in a "nicer, quieter neighborhood." On my twenty-fifth birthday, I invited him, not without many misgivings, to take supper with me. . . . (long afterward:) "It moved me profoundly," he said, "when you gave me a glass of milk, bread and butter, an egg, and a banana." It was the full measure of my festive birthday "spread"! "You were so simple and so solemn about it!" And I mused on it: to me, to have food enough was "party" enough. How vast was the distance between our two worlds!

◆ ◆ ◆

Miss Lockwood, Mr. Stokes and I made the trip to the Canadian camp together, sitting up in the coach all night, they for no other reason, I think, than that I was compelled to do so. I had only money enough for ordinary railroad tickets, and would not have known what to do with a berth had I been able to afford one.

Arrived at Cedar Lodge (July 29, 1904) after the long sleepless journey by train and boat, we were shown to our tents, to "wash up for breakfast." In I went to mine, and did not emerge till the morning of the following day: I slept all day and all night without once awakening.

Every guest and member of the household had been sent in rotation to discover whether I had yet stirred; but I slept and furnished excitement. At the breakfast table there was much good-natured laughter at my expense. I too laughed a bit, but thought: "They don't know—they don't know how close to collapse we are—always. They, with their stored-up energy, they who have not been wakened for years at dawn by the alarm clock, who have never worked in factories by day, and half the night in 'buckeyes' . . . They do not belong to my world, so cannot understand. To them it is merely funny. . . ." Olive Tilford Dargan (Fielding Burke) did not laugh. She understood. She knew! She knew poverty and struggle. We became fast friends, were in fact friends before meeting here, and our friendship has lasted throughout the years.

Neither did Mr. Stokes laugh. I marvelled that he should understand. But new love is old wisdom . . . In the evening we walked together, and talked of many things; and a close communion was born of that hour. The following day, skipping down an embankment to the lovely lake, I sprained my ankle. By and bye I chuckled and groaned. Was I not on vacation? . . . Crutches would have to come all the way from Quebec. In the meantime, Mr. Stokes, being also a surgeon (without a shingle) made a splint of a copy of the *Ladies' Home Journal*—there being nothing better at hand—and set my ankle. For several days, till the crutches came, I remained in a little summer-house down the hill by the margin of the lake, away from the center of camp. Nights, Olive Tilford Dargan slept in a cot beside mine. During the day, Mr. Stokes would come with a copy of Fitzgerald's translation of *The Light of Asia,* to read to me and to hear me read.[10] Here I learned much of his life—his youth at college, his studies in medicine because he wanted to "help the people"; of his discovery that "all disease has its root primarily in social causes"; of his leaving his father's house to live and work in the social settlements in order to "learn the causes of social ills and help to destroy them. . . ."

He talked of his dreams of the future—a future in which I was to share. . . . I contemplated the man; likened him to the young Buddha,

Siddhartha, in *The Light of Asia.* Siddhartha left his home, his fabulous Pleasure House and all that was near to him, to seek healing for the great ills of the world. . . . Was not he who sat before me also of that high race of men, consecrating his life to the service of mankind? Did not he, too, leave his father's mansion, renounce ease and luxury and a secluded life for life and work among the people? I sat in worship before him.

We were on high ground.

Behind us the camp; before us the lake, and the great hills, dark against a glowing sunset. We sat and talked of the future . . . "But Graham," I said, "you will be coming to my world, not I to yours . . . We will have a flat somewhere on the East Side, and live and work among the people. . . ."

With the gathering dusk, the daughter of our host, Mabel Hay Barrows, stole up quietly behind us—and laid on my brow a wreath of immortelles which she herself had plucked and woven. The friendly gesture moved me deeply, but it also embarrassed me. Do they suspect? Is our interest in each other so crassly obvious? I wanted it to be our secret, as yet. . . .

The following morning we left Cedar Lodge to fill another engagement. At sundown we arrived at "Summer Brook," the Adirondack camp of Mrs. Prestonia Mann Martin, at Hurricane, New York.

The John Martins were Fabians, and surrounded themselves with people of varying reform and revolutionary tendencies. They were lively hosts and their guests composed a group in character very like the groups that constantly visited the settlement. There were young guests good to look at and older guests good to hear. I looked and listened. I talked little. The great mountains (I had never seen mountains before) were a constant source of joy and wonder to me, and inspired the singing mood. So I would go off by myself and write "poetry." But the things of which I sang were not joyous things. When the clouds, "heavy with the weight of rains," hung low over the mountains, I likened them to

The pent-up hearts of the people,
heavy with planted seas
of terrible thunder and lightning.

There were many hours of discussion; social problems mainly. Someone projects a dream of the future—the free and equal society . . .
More discussion. I have no contribution to make. I simply sit and listen.
Someone discovers that I have written something about the "clouds and
the mountains." I am pressed to read it. I hang back. I am audience-
shy, but finally yield, and read my long effusion. It is a crude thing. The
guests are impressed. They try to draw me into discussion, but I fall quite
silent at this, then steal away. I like being by myself. . . .

The guests tramp. They climb White Face. Their feet twinkle hither
and yon. I play chess taught me by a Mr. Bloom, a friend of the family,
back in the Cleveland days. . . . I play chess with Charles Sprague
Smith, head of Cooper Union Institute.[11] My hostess watches the game
and chuckles: "You play a tenacious game. You never give up!" At times I
sit in some corner, my crutches beside me, my thoughts on the people—
the people and the future. I yearn for the day when somewhere on
the East Side, we shall live in a small flat and work for humanity. Our
engagement is not to be announced. We are to keep it secret for a while.
Only my mother will know. We will be married on my birthday, nearly
a year distant. Graham left for a few days on a visit to his family in their
Adirondack camp on Lake St. Regis. When he returned, he introduced
me, with the aid of the camera, to each member of his family. I gazed
long at those faces. Will we like each other? I wondered. Direct from
camp Graham went on a business trip, while I returned to New York
in the company of Maud Younger and Kellogg Durland, friends of the
University Settlement.

◆ ◆ ◆

When Graham and I spoke to my mother, she showed neither surprise nor excitement, but looked glad, and said quietly: "Well children,

there's a lot of work to be done. I hope you will be very happy—and useful."

We had resumed my work at the office and my activities at the Settlement. Before that winter was half spent, Graham had left for Mexico with his two maiden aunts, the Misses Olivia and Caroline Phelps Stokes. They had heard rumors of his interest in an "Israelitish maiden," and the trip was designed to provide him with a change of scene and—possibly of heart. Later however, they became friendly to me.

With the coming of Spring, July 18 seemed not so far away, so I gave up work at the office to return to the factory. Before anyone could know, I wanted to sit at the bench again, to renew the old labor, the old relationships. Perhaps I felt that never hereafter would my own regard me as one of them. "I will never change; but they—will they understand? After all, I shall become a rich man's wife," and I could not bear the thought that my marriage might prove a barrier between my class and me. I take a job in a cigar factory—somewhere between the sixties and seventies on Third Avenue.

It is good to be again among my own. We talk, we sing, we race—I am one of them. But I was a bit of a mystery to them. They cannot understand why I am there. They tell me so. "You ought to get a better kind of a job." "But why? Stogie rolling is good enough for me." "Well, you have a way about you—the way you talk and all— Why, you, you could even get work in a department store, if you tried. . . ." My hands swell from the unaccustomed movements. The fingers get puffed up. I cannot roll stogies now without great pain, but I stay on. At home I apply lotions. Graham calls, and notes my swollen hands, and insists on my staying out of the factory. After a few days, however, I return. But I am forced to get my last week's pay and to say goodbye. For, as I enter the loft, I am greeted with a din: Cutters rattle, knives beat on rolling-boards, shouts, calls, feet stamp, hands clap! I am bewildered. I can't understand this demonstration. Then one, a worker who has sat beside me, comes forward with a copy of the morning paper. It is all over the front page! I am recognized! I rush away with such phrases flung after me as "the luckiest girl in America! . . . Think of it! A millionaire! Don't forget us, Rose! Come to see us, sometimes." My face is burning. I feel a bit ashamed of their reactions.

◆ ◆ ◆

From that day on, our forthcoming marriage is a subject for daily headlining. We serve as an ever-renewable fairy-tale-come-true . . . the fairy-tale of "Democracy." Letters by the hundreds pile in upon us: congratulations, requests for autographs, pleas for help—And now that I am to "marry a millionaire," and am no longer a struggling unskilled worker in a stogie factory, I am invited to join the American Federation of Labor!!! Proposed by a Mr. Daniel S. Jacobs for membership in Cigarmakers Union Local No. 13 of New York and duly admitted.

Reporters pursue me. They come to my home, meet me on the street, waylay me on the "el." When I am not at home they see my mother. My poor mother complains, "What do the reporters want of me? When you are not here they come in anyway, and poke their noses into every corner. Pictures of you, of me, of the children . . . They look for your writings. May we have this, may we have that? They leave me no time to cook, to wash, to clean up."

"That's all right, Mamele. They are workers too, most of them underpaid and driven by need. It's not their fault. They hate to be a nuisance, but they are sent. Newspapers are no better than factories."

"What do they want with my life? Next time they come I'll send them flying."

"Don't send them away, Mamele. I'll talk to every one of them and give them anything they ask for."

"But what do they want with our private lives?"

"No life is private, Mother."

"I don't know what you mean, child. If millions of people who read the papers want to know what I am cooking in this little pot on my stove, this morning—"

"Then it is important that you tell them exactly what you are cooking. Whether we have or haven't enough to cook or too much is of great importance to everybody."

New burdens. Shopping; endless tramping about in the crowded shops; selecting materials; things to wear; fittings and again fittings at the dressmakers . . . I suppose one must go through all this; but I tire. Graham's sisters, Helen and Ethel, are friendly and helpful. They are charged with preparing my trousseaux. I know nothing of what to get and where to get it. I never stand beside them in the shops as they select the finery, the materials for dresses, the costly accessories, without wondering why it is needful—since I am to live on the East Side. In my world, I think to myself, there is no need for such things. And I shall go my own way.

• • •

"Brick House" is the family estate. It is on Collender's Point, Noroton, Connecticut. From "Brick House" I am to be married. Here I am brought for rest in the early summer. Helen is with us. I like Helen and am pleased to be so much with her. But I am not resting. The sunken rose garden, the walks, the terraces, the belvederes, the pier and the boats, the shining waters of Long Island Sound beyond great shade trees that had been brought in and planted full-grown, the wide velvet lawns—they should give me joy. But all the beauty of the scene, the sweetness of the air, the color and odor of the flowers, gripped my heart like a hand of steel. I watched the gardeners; simple workers; blameless people like my step-father—a whole corps of them—tending the thousands of blooms; trimming the rare shrubbery; making smooth the fine gravel paths; laboring to keep the tennis courts in perfect condition; bending with bodies that can no longer stand straight in the sun; making with gnarled fingers paradise for a few . . . And I weep. As I watch them, I see Madison Street; see the East Side; the city with its millions of workers; my fellow-workers in the Cleveland cigar factory; and I weep and wonder where so many tears come from! Indoors, I wander about the vast mansion, through its spacious halls; its enormous drawing-room; other rooms; upstairs; down. I move from treasure to treasure in room after room and think and weep. Graham expected me to be awed, delighted. "But, dear, you surprise me," he says. And I to him: "I have conceived of more beautiful mansions—in a new world. I have not needed to live in them to imagine them; mansions made for workers—by and for those who build and make all things useful and beautiful. The breadmakers and the brick-makers; the music-makers and the portrait painters; the peasants and the weavers; the shoemakers; the teachers; the scientists; tailors; fishermen; cooks and singers—serving the common need; enjoying the common wealth." I sometimes grow eloquent. . . .

A corps of servants for an empty house—a house in which forty guests can be comfortably accommodated, beside the servants, beside the numerous family at present traveling in Europe. For many months of the year—an empty house! And so many servants caring for so empty a house! How can I—who had often to sleep on a pallet in a corner of the kitchen—find rest and recreation here? I, knowing what I know! I belonged to the gardeners, the servants, the stablemen, the mechanics, they who lived insecure lives saving what miserable little they can against the day when sickness or unemployment leaves them helpless. I never sink into a chair or upon a sofa with its rich coverings of brocade, without feeling startlingly alive to the contrast between these and the hard backless benches of the factory.

Sometimes, I go and sit in the quiet library to escape the things that hurt in the rest of the house. Here are solemn row upon row of finely bound books behind glass doors. I go from one case to another searching for something to read. Nothing here to tell me what I seek to know— how the poor can do away with their poverty. These books are about great men, mostly—great governors; presidents; legislators; generals; Napoleon; Wellington; Washington; the great "captains of industry." I search vainly for the story of Us—the Peoples, and close the glass doors safely upon the great. Other times I sit here for several hours acknowledging gifts and writing cards to wedding guests. The spirit of the books disturbs me. The volumes seem to leap from their places and to assail me with proud assertions: "We are the Few, the Rich, the Powerful! What can you do against us—you and your poor, you and your Many!" "Nevertheless," I think, "nevertheless, we will abolish poverty, despite you." And again I am tormented with questions of how. I escape the library by going to the billiard room with Graham.

At times, I leave the dinner table in the midst of a meal. The tears well up and I cannot control them. The contrasts are so sharp; they stab like knife-thrusts. The silver service, the costly glassware, the food; course after course of the best, the richest, the rarest! Memories sweep over me of toil and hunger and the panic of 1903. . . . "Because I no longer work," I think, "because I have come into the world that lives on the toil of others, I get all this!" The thought that in October we shall be in a little flat on Norfolk Street, among my people, working for a new day, comforts me.

Arrangements for the wedding are being completed. I am barely interested, hardly aware. Graham comes to discuss final considerations with me. "Yes, Graham," I say, "everything is all right. It doesn't really matter." On the inspiration of the moment I add, "but I want the word 'obey' eliminated from the service." The request has upset plans somewhat. The local minister has refused to conduct the service. He cannot leave out "obey." Such a thing has never been done before! He will not take the responsibility. There are family councils. J.G.'s brother, Anson Phelps Stokes, Jr., Secretary of Yale University, is also a minister. He will conduct the service. I literally ran up the aisle and down again, I was told. Perhaps I did. It was something disagreeable to be gone through with, quickly. . . .

It was a mixed company at the wedding reception at Brick House. My beloved Mrs. Shapiro was there and Sonya Levien[12] who brought me back to the Settlement; and many of our Settlement friends; and my beloved Mamele with the children; and Flora Mayer (Mrs. Henry Rauh), matron of honor; and a large company from that other world beside the numerous members of the groom's family—including his parents, who returned from Europe several days before the wedding and W.E.D. Stokes, the "scapegrace" of the family, who, on this occasion, became reconciled to his brother, Anson Phelps Stokes, the father of the groom. Apparently a happy company, mixing well. Yet I am never for a moment unconscious of class differences . . .

The wedding guests eat and drink, and talk and laugh. The tables are set on the wide terrace; the awnings are spread, the servants flit about among the guests pouring from long dark bottles into broad-bowled slender-stemmed glasses a pale golden liquid. A very popular drink, it seems. Glasses are filled and re-filled. Barton, the family butler, brings a bottle to our table. "Have some, Rosalie," Graham urges. I gaze at the stuff being poured out for me, the guests near us smile and I wonder what is wrong.

"But what is this?" I ask.

"Ginger-ale," says someone nearby.

"Oh." I lift the glass to my lips, take a sip, and screw up my face and set the glass back on the table. "I don't like this kind of ginger-ale," I say. Later I learn it was champagne, and I am glad that, without knowing, I didn't like it. . . .

I am in a grey tailored suit, dressed for traveling. Graham comes and stands beside me, as I gaze from an upper window across the western bay.

"You know, dear, we will want a home—a place we can rest and expand in. We'll build."

"A home? Yes, I suppose . . ."

"Where would you like to live, dear?"

In the bay, lies a little green island. I wave toward it.

"Islands must be happy places," I muse. "Maybe there . . ."

"If it can be procured," says Graham, "we shall have it."

◆ ◆ ◆

We sail on the "Cedric," July 19, 1905. My mother-in-law had left her Packard for our use abroad. With what eagerness I looked forward to visiting London! And again with what mingled emotions I looked again upon Black Lion's yard! Here was the house, where my father tried to be a boss and could not. There, the very lamp-post under which I stopped the white-haired man who walked with naked feet on the icy paving-stones. I looked for the sweets' shop, second door to my left coming out of the yard on to Whitechapel. It was not there. It would long since have disappeared. And how narrow and mean the Yard that had been so wide and long to a child of ten years! I stood in the middle of the yard and stretched out both my arms. I could almost touch the walls of the houses on either side!

We drive to Red Lion Court. I want to see again the place where I danced Irish jigs with "Reddy," to see again the room where my mother and I made black satin bows for ladies' slippers. As we approached the court, I become aware of a group of women near the very door to the old house. Prepared by the London press that heralded our coming apparently, they are organized to receive us! I am too conscious of the automobile, of Henri the chauffeur, of my custom-tailored costume and my fine black straw hat with its ostrich plume. . . . Why the cost of merely what we have on our backs can ransom any one of these working women from care! I cannot enter the court. Graham too is disinclined to go further. We get back into the car and drive away.

"Seven Chambord Street." My mother had given me the address—had folded my hand upon the slip of paper with warm pressure of both her hands. Henri stops the car a block away and we walk to Number Seven. I find my little Aunt Esther and the children, and my Uncle Solomon again. Glowing with the warmth of them, I forget the vague little shadow, indefinable, saddening—that has crept over me . . . "Oh my dear ones, my very dear ones!" I embrace and kiss them, again and again. But how mean and small, how cramped and dark and close the quarters! So many bodies to live and breathe within such narrow walls, beneath these low ceilings and my Uncle Solomon so starved-looking and ill! . . . Fresh from wide ocean spaces, the effect upon me is staggering. Before we leave, I get Graham's promise to pay their passage to New York. At least they might live near my mother. (They came that year. But my Uncle Solomon did not survive. He died in a New York hospital, in the year following.) We found my Aunt Sarah too. Her teeth are almost eaten away. She looked ill and old. Uncle Rosenthal, a startling whiteness on his face and greyish cast over his eyes, stands tall and straight, and proud and silent. I cannot bear the agony of that silent figure . . . A lovely little granddaughter comes in, she is fawn-like, with russet hair that clusters adorably around her head . . . How can I leave them and go away? If they too might come . . . But "We can't bring them all," says Graham, looking hurt to say it. "Of course," I think, "I am unreasonable, I suppose." Graham bends low as we leave the doorway, and I trail after, my heart near to breaking. As we get into the limousine I feel as if I had this moment thrust out a hand, fingers out-spread, and pushed a beloved, appealing face under water, and made off in a snug little boat. . . .

England, Wales, Scotland, the Continent, galleries, old castles and ruins, quaint Welsh hamlets, the highlands of Scotland long-loved in song, seen now abloom with the purple heather; Paris, the Louvre with its thousands of dreams of beauty in canvas, marble, bronze. Strange, feathery, rose-tipped cloud at sunset that proves to be Mont Blanc, and brings me in the moving car to my feet with a great shout. The Bay of Naples, Rome, and again galleries; a bewildering wealth of art. I drink of it all. But down in the grass market in Edinburgh I saw the poor, the workers, on Saturday night.

In Italy Graham and I stand before a Donatello. "What a lovely boy!" says Graham. I think of the homeless man I saw in the grass market with a baby in his arms—at midnight, being turned away from charity shelter—ruled out because of the child, walking into the night, hugging his baby close . . . and I saw his eyes. . . . "Yes, a lovely boy! . . . Life lies bleeding and Art smiles."

◆ ◆ ◆

Now we are again in New York and on the East Side. We begin furnishing our flat and get to work. But before we could bring any furnishings into the little apartment on the top floor of the house on the northwest corner of Norfolk and Grand Streets we entertained many visitors. The first to call was John Burns, Member of Parliament, who came when we could offer him only a candle stuck in a saucer for light, and a packing-case for a seat. I recall him chiefly for this circumstance. As a reformer he had nothing to offer, and seemed to have no faith in his own creed. Though he stayed for two hours or more, he left with me only a flat impression.[13]

By the time we had a desk, a table, several chairs and Graham's books from the Settlement installed in the alcove of the front room, a stream of up-towners had called and left their cards. My tray was soon piled high with these dainty bits of cardboard. But I had no taste or time for "teas," and was determined never to be drawn into the world of idle women and exploiting men. As a result of our being continually headlined in the press, our mail became so heavy it literally overwhelmed us. Appeals, congratulations, requests of all kinds—from money to advice, from "audiences" to autographs; while hundreds of big fat envelopes streamed in, containing schemes for saving the world. These were usually hand-written and hard to decipher. Working at the desk often till late in the night, I was still unable to keep abreast of this correspondence. Friends and family laughed: "They are only cranks. Ignore them." But I, at any rate, could not. They were so much in earnest, they had to be answered. Finally, Sonya Levien came to be our private secretary, to share the burden of desk work. Letters, articles, interviews—these were only a part of the overcrowded day. Neighbors and the needy came—a constant stream. Often, I forgot to eat, went without food all day till I grew faint. The reporters were almost as numerous as neighbors. They came early in the morning, they came at noon, at night; telephoned and shook me out of sleep in the wee hours. They were always welcomed.

Graham was drawn into politics. The Municipal Ownership League —Hearst's League, as it was popularly called—William Randolph Hearst for Mayor, J. G. Phelps Stokes for President of the Board of Aldermen. . . . I was not happy about it.

And what strange political bed fellows! One day, during the campaign, a Mrs. Henry Seigel called. She stood near a window facing Grand Street, and commented insolently on the working girls in the street below. The Seigels were of the Seigel and Cooper store on Sixth Avenue. Their working girls lived in poverty but they themselves lived up-town in a fine house. Only at Graham's urging did I go to the luncheon she came to invite me to. There were possibly twenty guests at the long table. A Bishop Potter,[14] an unctious [sic] gentleman, sat on my right. Mr. Hearst sat somewhat to my left. I knew little about the man. He looked kindly and clean-cut, and I wished he were a socialist. Mrs. Hearst, whom I observed later in the drawing-room, was a beautiful woman. But all the women, including Mrs. Hearst, were gorgeously decked out. The place was oppressive with flunkeys, jewels, extravagant display. I took no part in conversation, thinking over and over, "What have I—a worker, to do here? How can these people want a solution to our problems?"

When the campaign was in full swing and the East Side in a ferment of agitation, I was sad over the possible outcome, and kept wishing for Graham's defeat. One evening, passing my living-room window, I heard Graham's name flung upward from the street below. I leaned out to see. A very fiery young man was making a speech from a soapbox on the corner. A little knot of men, women and children had collected about him. He was pointing up at my window—at me. He was saying things about us. I strained to hear . . . "Municipal Ownership is no solution" he cried, "so long as the propertied classes own the municipalities. J. G. Phelps Stokes is a rich man—a man of property; he belongs to the capitalist class. The Municipal Ownership League is a rich man's creation. W. R. Hearst belongs in the millionaire class. This is his government. He doesn't want to change his government. The Socialist Party is the workers' party, and what we want is a government of, for, and by the people who work." "Hear, hear!" I called down, leaning far out of the window and clapping my hands.

Every evening, while J. G. was campaigning for the Municipal Ownership League, I sat at the window and listened to the fiery soap-boxer Jacob Panken, today the Honorable Jacob Panken, who supports the "Municipal Ownership" he then denounced.[15]

• • •

The poor, the sick, the needy, the suffering—they come at all hours. I love them. I would give them my life. Early—often before I am up, they open the door which I never lock, and walk in. At times, they walk straight from the kitchen (which is entered from the hall) into my bedroom to the left. They sit on the edge of my bed and unburden their sorrows to me. Often, my tears mingle with theirs. . . .

I help where I can. But I begin to realize that helping in this way is like pouring water through a sieve. I am still at the Settlement. I am also on the Local Committee of the Charity Organization Society. Here, I flatter myself, I—being a worker, may be able to heal where the up-towner only hurts. I work with enthusiasm. But "cases" bring their own logic.

One day the Committee assigned me to an Italian family. The man had developed tuberculosis. The Society wanted to send him to a hospital, but he could not be persuaded to leave his home. Possibly, I might succeed where others had failed. They would have me try. I found the wretched tenement on Grand Street near the East River, climbed up two dark flights of stairs, and entered the one sunless room they called "home." The wife was bending over a sick baby in a crib while two tots tugged at her skirts. The room had only two windows. Both looked north and were sealed tightly—to save the precious warmth from the few bits of coal in the cook-stove. As I entered, a cadaverous man with silken black hair and black eyes in cadaverous sockets, rose and came from his seat near a window. A sudden coldness greeted the "charity lady." But when I gave them my name they drew me warmly to a chair. "Oh, yes, you too were a worker. . . ." Between coughing spells—sharp, dry, the man told me—with a fierce eagerness in his labored speech— of the years of struggle here; of the long work-days; the short rations; the miserable pay; the wretched life. . . . "Always I live like this," he flamed, sweeping a claw-like hand over the miserable room. "Never enough eat, never enough rest, no air, no sunshine. I give America everything I got—and what America give me—me and my wife and my children? Poverty, sickness, consumption! I wanta no charity, I wanta joostice."

I flamed too. He was my class brother. His plea was my plea. How absurd that I should be there representing "Charity"! I flamed too and talked long to them both. Could but the Society have heard me! . . . As I turned to go I caught a glimpse of a photograph on the mantel-shelf. "Who is that?" I could not but ask. Such a beautiful face, such glorious health and strength. "Dat was me," said the man, "dat wasa me when I come to this country. . . ."

I resigned from the Charity Organization Society.

Through Graham's sister Ethel (Mrs. John Sherman Hoyt) I had attended several meetings of the National Flower Guild. She wanted so much to have me "see the work" they were doing. The meeting was in the home of Mrs. James Speyer, 257 Madison Avenue. Wealthy women were supplying the poor in the tenements with window-boxes "at a very low price," and sending their no-longer-fresh boudoir bouquets to the sick in the hospital wards. The spectacle filled me with a fierce impatience. Ladies putting gay if half-faded frills around the festering sores of the working class—and I permit myself to be drawn into these gatherings. I determine to seek out workers' organizations. Often, Graham asks, "Why so sad, Rosalie?" "Socialism," I answer.

We attend meetings, conferences; reformistic, socialistic. My enthusiasm for settlement work waned. I perceived that the groups which provide the funds and dominate the policies of the social settlements frown upon all socialism . . . seek only to content the workers with a little "culture." "Settlements afford no meeting-place to workers seeking to change the base of society. They are like the Charity Organization Society," I maintained, "helping the poor" in order to keep them "in their place," that is "in poverty." And J.G. concurred in this.

There were dinners of the Collectivist Society. I also attended meetings of the Women's Trade Union League. A Cigar Makers Committee was formed to organize the girls in the cigar factories. Nothing came of it. Still, I was not discouraged and continued to attend the League meetings. I went to hearings in City Hall on questions affecting tenement conditions. I came away with the feeling that in such places a game is being played by "public" officials in the interest of the rich landlords; the merchants; the public utility corporations; and capitalists generally. I attended a few lectures on Bernard Shaw, that winter. My first acquaintance with him; an idol breaker who did me good.

◆ ◆ ◆

Graham was a member of the Board of Directors of Tuskegee Institute, so it was natural for me to be on the special train which carried a body of distinguished men and women to Alabama to the celebration of its twenty-fifth anniversary (April 1906). Nor was it strange that on the way I should find myself seated vis-a-vis with one of the distinguished gentlemen. This gentleman happened to be none other than Dr. Charles William Eliot, President Emeritus of Harvard University.[16]

Dr. Eliot was bland, communicative before he began to question me. Then he became an entirely different personality. It seems that he wanted to know about my speed in the factory. Was I a very quick worker? Yes, very quick. Was I not naturally quick? Yes, naturally. Supposing you had worked slowly, would you not have been unhappy? I suppose so, but—It would have been impossible for you to work other than rapidly, would it not? Well—yes, but I—It hurts a naturally quick worker to work slowly, does it not? Yes, but you see—

Each time I tried to explain further, I was interrupted. I wanted to tell him how Need drove me, and how my boss drove me—much faster than my fresh energies and the natural fleetness of my fingers warranted, but somehow, I could not; somehow, I was not allowed. I wanted to tell him too how my speed snapped in the end, but he would not let me proceed—always interposed a question—quickly, smoothly; till I felt convinced he would let me go no further than to tell him what he wanted me to tell him. When finally I arose and left him to approaching friends, I felt like a "green" witness leaving the witness stand after being in the hands of a very clever prosecuting attorney: I had greatly misrepresented my own case without being able to help myself.

"Curious," I thought. "Such a great educator! Isn't he interested in learning the *whole* truth of the matter. . . ."

On the way south I fell ill with a heavy cold—strangely enough, just as we came into the warm, sunny southern air. Someone sent me a posie. It was Mr. Andrew Carnegie. (Mr. and Mrs. Carnegie were also of the party.) I felt queer about it, for I had read of Homestead.[17] When we got to Tuskegee, I had occasion to see and hear Mr. Carnegie. He made a number of speeches—told students and guests what are the qualities that make for success. To my best recollection the outstanding qualities to his mind, as stressed in these speeches were: Patriotism, Personality, Perseverance. Looking upon the jolly, child-like little Scotchman I found it hard to connect him with the brutalities and cruelties for which his partner, Mr. Henry Clay Frick nearly paid for with his life at the hands of the protesting Alexander Berkman. Still, I remembered as I listened to Mr. Carnegie that Shakespeare had warned me not to read a man's character in his countenance.

While at Tuskegee, I had occasion to get a closer view of Mr. Carnegie. In a mischievously communicative mood, he joined a group of us and began telling stories of his early life. Among them was one about an early contract. The city of St. Louis was building a bridge. The bridge required steel of "two thousand moduli of elasticity." The city had applied to a number of steel men then in the field but none of them could contract to produce the steel called for. The city of St. Louis then wrote Mr. Carnegie. Could he produce steel of "two thousand moduli of elasticity"? And, if he could would he please say what such steel would cost the city of St. Louis. "I hadn't the least idea what steel of 'two thousand moduli of elasticity' meant," chuckled Andrew Carnegie. "But I wrote St. Louis undertaking to deliver steel of 'two thousand moduli of elasticity.' But, I added, steel of 'two thousand moduli of elasticity' will cost you—well, I named a fabulous figure. I got the contract, and they did not get the 'two thousand moduli of elasticity'!"

Good-natured laughter followed in the group. "But, Mr. Carnegie," came a friendly voice, "how did you get away with it?"

Mr. Carnegie seemed to be waiting for this query. A broad grin spread over the elf-like face; his little eyes twinkled, his funny little nose wrinkled up and flattened out; he was the picture of impish delight as he added the crowning bit to his story.

"Well, I had a nephew in Scotland at the time who was an engineer. When I wrote St. Louis closing the contract, I wrote my nephew asking him to explain to me what is 'two thousand moduli of elasticity,' and can it be produced. I knew that if it could be produced I would produce it, and if it could not the law would not hold me to it. Well—it couldn't be produced. And I made two million dollars on that deal."

Later: When the group had disbanded: "Clever of him, wasn't it? . . ." "Oh, he's an astute industrialist!" etc., etc., etc.

Toward the end of the celebration at Tuskegee, the guests were gathered in one room looking at some paintings. I no longer recall what occasioned the remark—but Mr. Carnegie who was standing beside me, put a hand on my arm and inclined my ear. "Shsh!" he whispered. "Don't tell anyone! But I don't believe in God."

Through the trip south I kept Graham in distress because I insisted that I would go and sit in the "Colored" instead of the "white" waiting-room, whenever the train stopped. Confronted with Jim-Crowism for the first time, I could not bear the indignity to black workers. "I'll go and sit where they sit," was the natural thing for me to say. "Don't, please don't," Graham pleaded, "It will do no good in the world, and you'll only succeed in getting yourself arrested." And I would retort, "I want to be arrested, if that is the case." So, when Graham announced that we were going with the Carnegie party (Mr. Carnegie had asked a small number of the Tuskegee party to join him) to share the luncheon to be given in his honor at the opening of the new Carnegie Library in Atlanta, I did not realize that I would leave that luncheon in protest against Jim-Crowism.[18] The "best people" in Atlanta were gathered in the upper hall of the shining white Library building. And what an impressive stairway we trod to reach the upper hall! But we had barely joined that select company when someone whispered to me that "dogs and Negroes are not allowed in this building." Whereupon "I won't stay!" I said to Graham and we both walked out and left the building that would not admit Negroes.

On the sidewalk before the imposing Carnegie Library stood Oswald Garrison Villard with Mrs. Villard, and young Mr. [Edward Twichell] Ware, who succeeded his father to the presidency of Atlanta University. At Tuskegee I had been told that Mr. Ware was barred for accepting the presidency of a Negro institution of learning (as had his father before him) from every socially prominent white man's home in Atlanta. So we stopped to talk to Mr. Ware and the Villards who were also of the Tuskegee party. Then, Mr. Ware hailed a cab, and the five of us drove to Atlanta University, I weeping all the way for the sorrows of the Southern black man. For I had not yet learned to translate my sympathies and my protest into anything more effective than tears.

At the university we addressed a group of Negro students, then took a train back to New York.

CHAPTER IV

Campaigning for Socialism

We returned home only till I could recover from my bronchial attack, then started west. Graham made a semi-annual trip to Nevada, where he had "mining and railroad interests." This time, he suggested, he would take me with him, and I was glad to go. The plan was to go from the mines clear to the coast and spend a week in San Francisco. But the Great Earthquake came while we were on the way, and modified our plan. We spent the time in Pasadena instead. Fortunately. For here we met and heard one of the most stirring speakers on the socialist platform—J. Stitt Wilson.[1] His message (on May 1, and several times thereafter) was so vitally delivered that I had no peace of mind till, three months later, I joined the Socialist Party. Many, many times on the way back to New York Graham would interrupt my brooding with the same question: "What is it, Rosalie, Socialism?" Indeed, I could think of nothing else. Every waking hour was occupied with the same thought—The Party! I sought out meetings, made individual contacts, bought pamphlets. . . .

Meanwhile, influences from the Municipal Ownership League were at work on J.G. He confided to me that he was approached with the proposal that if he would stay with the Municipal Ownership League he would receive the nomination for the Governorship of the State of

New York. When it appeared to me that he was seriously considering it, I put up the most determined opposition, and took every opportunity when we were together to press the question of his resignation from the Municipal Ownership League, and of our joining the Socialist Party. Finally, he told me he was ready to take the step in favor of Socialism. Letters were drafted—of resignation from the Municipal Ownership League (August 1, 1906) and application at the same time in the Socialist Party.

Our applications were joyously accepted. We received our red cards with rejoicing, and were pressed without delay into the State campaign. John Chase was the S.P. candidate for Governor, and the party mapped a tour for the three of us, covering every possible town in the State—even hamlets where lone sympathizers were willing and able to arrange meetings.[2] Then Chase, Graham and I went forth to make converts.

I have often thought back to that first campaign. John Chase was always amusing. He seemed more entertainer than campaigner. He would tell the funniest stories, and keep the audience in stitches. While Graham had every advantage of education, and having beside studied socialism closely for a number of years, was the "intellectual," the educator. I had no time to study much from books, as yet; but I could, and did, bring my years of experience as a worker to my audiences.

From the very first (and with few exceptions over a period of twenty years) I made no notes and had no set speech. I coined my words as I stood and faced the audience. Speeches differed in approach as my audiences differed, and had to come "fresh from the mint." I preferred struggling through, to studying oratory. "Workers want to be told," I would say, "they don't want orations. Better tell them simply, if awkwardly, than study to make an effect." The few "orations" I had heard that were intended to move one to tears had moved me to laughter rather. I determined to learn to think on my feet. . . . But I never learned to rise to my feet with confidence. Once I started speaking this feeling would leave me quite. But before I began I suffered intensely. With a few shining exceptions, my twenty years on the platform in which I made thousands of speeches, proved that I had no cause for this feeling of uncertainty. But I never failed to be in a fever from the moment I got into the hall, or long before, until I rose to face my audiences and actually began to speak—always certain that I shall be unable to think on my feet. Over that long period of years my speeches were uneven, of course. At times I spoke fairly well, at others poorly or very badly; a speech that pleased an audience—as I would afterward learn, would keep me awake half the night, aching for having "missed my opportunity," or, it would be the other way around. Graham often teased: "Whenever you are most certain that you are going to fail, you are sure to make a fine speech." That was not infrequently the case. But every test was an ordeal by fire.

During that first campaign, as in later ones in which Graham took part, I would sit and listen to him with the most complete concentration, yet suffering hot and cold spells, certain of my failure when my turn came to speak. Nevertheless, it was a profound joy to me to be able to reach so many workers with the message that for years I had burned to bring them. Even my youthful desire to "sing for thousands" was a desire to reach the people with the songs of the people—the folk and labor songs that might stir them and be for them a unifying force.

We had many interesting meetings in that first campaign. Two of these however, I have particular reason to recall. One was in Ithaca, at Cornell University, the other at a little town called Watervleit. The one at the university is remembered for an experience connected with it that is unique in my life. The one at Watervleit I recall for its own sake.

Well along in the campaign we were due at Ithaca, but I became quite ill just before train time, and felt that I could not go on. Both men were greatly troubled. They could not leave me behind, and the meeting at the university was one important enough not to be lightly cancelled. But John Chase brightened. He had an idea. "I know what will fix you up, Comrade Stokes," he said, "an egg-nog." I was in great pain, but grew hopeful hearing of a remedy that sounded harmless enough. "All right," I said as cheerfully as I could, "anything that will help us all get to the meeting." So the three of us walked till we found a cafe. "Here," said John Chase, "I'm sure we can get an egg-nog." So we walked in.

It was a quiet, genteel sort of dining place—not the kind of proletarian places we often found in the workers' sections. There were many little tables with white cloths, and shaded with dainty lamps in soft rose. We sat down at one of these tables, and Comrade Chase did the ordering, while Graham studied some notes, and I moaned a bit, unable to contain myself despite the very formal people who sat at a table across the room.

Presently, a waiter came and placed a tall tumbler before me. It was filled with a hot, yellowish liquid, and had a queer, strong odor.

"What is it made of, Comrade," I asked Chase.

"Oh, egg and milk and things," said John Chase. "Drink it down steadily while it's hot."

So I drank it down as directed, though I did not relish its peculiar flavor. It was not many minutes when I seemed to feel better. In a little while I felt still better. Then I began to feel much, much better than I had any right in all propriety to feel. I felt so good, in fact, that I began to laugh from sheer sense of well-being—then giggled—and giggled . . . Poor Graham was mortified, and begged me over and over to stop. But though I half-realized his reaction I could not contain myself. I felt so relaxed and released . . . Finally Graham and my contrite "medical advisor" led me away to the "Ladies Sitting Room" where I sank upon a soft, heavenly couch and went promptly to sleep.

After an hour, still aching, but with the additional disadvantage of a headache—an ailment to which I was quite unused, I boarded the train with my fellow-campaigners, and went to Ithaca, and directly to the meeting. I pleaded illness. But nobody at the meeting in the university really knew why I made my speech *seated* before my audience.

The meeting at Watervleit found us all very, very sober. When we arrived at Watervleit rain was coming down in torrents. To use the vernacular, it was raining "cats and dogs." In the face of such weather the question arose whether we ought to stay in Watervleit, or go on to the next town for the next day's meeting. What! Miss an opportunity to talk to workers? I would not hear of it. Was there any likelihood of a meeting being held on such a day, in a place like Watervleit? "There won't be a baker's dozen," said Chase. "Let there be a baker's half-dozen." I maintained we should talk to them nevertheless. Later, the deluge still beating down at Watervleit, the three of us trudged to the hall. Naturally, we found a very small meeting-room. And it was filled with empty rows of backless long, wooden benches, that faced an improvised speakers' stand. On one of these benches we three sat and waited. We waited a long time. Finally, one man walked in, then another. Then one of the two came over and consulted with us. He was the chairman. Should he open the meeting and introduce the speakers, or should he call it off? "Call off the meeting! By no means!" I interposed. "We'll speak— yes, each one of us! Why not?" So we sat and waited a little longer. By-and-bye, the doors opened and a third man came in. This seemed to encourage the Comrade Chairman; so, he opened the meeting and introduced the speakers, one by one, and after each introduction he was kind and thoughtful enough to take a seat up front—to swell the audience. . . .

As we walked away from the hall, somewhere near eleven o'clock, I quoted Swinburne with a happy chuckle: "While three men hold together, the kindgoms are less by three."

Since that autumn evening twenty-five years ago, I have at times addressed audiences of thirty thousand, but never with greater zeal or earnestness than when I talked to that audience of three in Watervleit, New York, in the campaign of 1906.

◆ ◆ ◆

My understanding took a leap forward in the year of crisis 1907–08.

It was a bad winter. In the old days I thought in terms of my own need and the need of the little world about me. But now—my growing knowledge of socialism made thinking in units impossible for me. I was compelled to think in terms of millions.

"Hard Times," said the workers. "Under-consumption," said the Socialists. "Over-production," said the capitalists. Several million workers
were walking the streets of the richest country in the world—hungry,
penniless, seeking work that was not to be had anywhere. Here was
the same thing happening that had happened to us in our early days in
America—shortly after my stepfather had been lured here by American
Agencies. ("Come! Plenty of work to be had, only—come!) Here was
something happening that had happened to us in Cleveland in 1893. . . .
I could still see my boss as he took me to the doors of the stockroom,
flung them wide and said, "Look! look!" A vast space with shelves that
reached to the high ceiling, with racks that filled the large floor and
rose to the very top of the room bursting with the cigars and stogies we
had made—that we had been driven ten and twelve hours a day and
overtime to make; packed—and waiting; waiting—for what? Waiting
to be bought; to be used up, consumed, "enjoyed." . . . Yes, the same
thing that had happened to us in 1893 when the boss said, "No work
now. When I get rid of the stock on hand you may come back." And
when everywhere we went we got the same answer: "After we get rid of
the surplus come back, and we'll give you work." But without work, we
can buy no food, and without food . . . ?

I re-lived the un-nameable agony of that crisis. What it did to my
kind step-father. What it did to all of us and to the simple hardworking
blameless folk about us. Here was a new crisis and I struggled to understand the matter, to tell it to the other workers—the tens of thousands
that now I was able to reach. Already I knew something of the past,
that in my grandfather's day workmen owned their own tools because
tools were simple and easy to get, and the steam-driven tool had not yet
come into existence; I knew that then men worked hard and had little
enough for their labor, but no man could say to them, "I will not let you
work. You shall starve until I can get rid of your product at a profit to
me." I had seen my Uncle Solomon forced to lay down his hand tools
when the power-driven machines came to his industry and the masters

took possession of them. He could not compete with those machines and live. I remembered his long search for work; the hunger, the despair. Now I saw millions like my Uncle Solomon begging work from those who by hook or by crook had gotten control of the machinery of production. . . . All now goes to the owners of the machines—for the right to work—just for the right to work which is the right to live! And for this labor what does he receive? A very small part of what they produce, barely enough to keep going.

In the old days at the bench I used to wonder how it is that we get so little when we produce so much? Now my growing knowledge of Socialism gave me the answer. The process ran through my head in some such way as the following:

Capitalism:

The bosses own and control industry for their private profit, not for human use. Therefore, they use every technical advance, every economy in industry, not to shorten hours of labor, and increase wages, but to throw men out of work.

This increases the army of workless men.

The growing army stands outside the factory gates begging for the right to work at any wage that will hold body and breath together.

The bosses are glad to see many men looking for work. Up to a certain point, a growing workless army helps the bosses to force down wages.

Men at work can be counselled to accept anything that despairing men without work are forced by starvation to work for.

The bosses use the unemployed as a club over the heads of the employed workers: so that, no matter what vast wealth the workers create, they suffer starvation and semi-starvation both sides of the industrial gates!

What then becomes of the vast surplus?—the bosses' pure profit?

What becomes of it, since the workers may not touch a thread or a grain more than their wages will buy back?

The Rich are limited, despite their wasteful extravagance. They cannot eat or drink more than or wear more than time or space will allow.

They cannot live in more than one house at a time, even though they keep several boarded up for use in the rounds of the seasons.

What becomes of the vast abundance—what happens to it all?

The very same thing that happened to our cigars and stogies: The product piled up.

Our product belongs to the boss.

Our product is his legal property. . . .

It is what's left between the miserable little that we are allowed to consume and the extravagant much that the capitalist class consumes and wastes.

It represents the bosses' pure profit; it's what they've built the system for: their profit.

We workers need all the good things we have made.

But the bosses will not give them back to us.

And since we can buy back but little or nothing with low wages or none, the bosses look for other people in other lands—somewhere, anywhere in the world upon whom to unload our products at a profit.

In the meantime, they shut down the gates of industry.

In the meantime, millions of us hunger.

In the meantime, other millions work three days and hunger four.

In the meantime, the bosses cut wages.

In the meantime, deeper misery grips the working class. . . .

Nothing to be done about it, say the bosses; Wait—wait till we are rid of the surplus. . . . Wait!

"Hard Times!" cry the workers, not knowing they are robbed in the mills, the mines, and the factories.

"Under-consumption!" cry the Socialists, trying to know how we are robbed.

"Over-production!" wail the capitalists, trying to blind us to the robbery.

What then happens to the piled-up products—what, while we hunger and suffer for the lack of it all?

Part of it rots.

Part is deliberately destroyed by the bosses to keep up prices.

In the main, it stays piled up—mountain-high!

Throughout the length and breadth of the land storerooms, warehouses, granaries burst with the good and necessary things that our hands have made. . . . But we go hungry; we suffer.

The bosses and their Government say we may not use our products.

They turn the police like dogs upon us. Their courts, their Law—all the force and violence of the Capitalist State, they use against us if we dare to lay hands upon our own: even to a loaf of bread; even to a bottle of milk for a starving child!

In the meantime, they rush hither and yon, madly seeking a way out—a way to get rid of the Surplus we have created and they have kept.

They dare not delay too long.

True, they need an unemployed army to keep down wages.

But too great an army threatens the life of their system.

Too great an army will break down the locked gates of industry.

Too great an army will take possession of the tools of life.

Too great an army will put an end to the rule of the bosses and secure to all men work and bread and life!

Dare the bosses rest until they get rid of the Surplus?—at a profit— always, of course, at a profit?

No, they dare not rest.

They are tormented day and night, night and day, by one problem— one only:

How to save themselves and continue to enslave us.

And they have but one solution:

WAR!

War is their one escape.

And their Government, responsive to the needs of the capitalist class, prepares for, declares, conducts, and drives the workers into war *for the sole purpose* of opening up to our bosses new and profitable markets for our products. . . .

We, the workers, are driven to slaughter to help our masters exploit new lands and enslave new masses, in order that they may use again on the old terms those of us that survive, in order that they may again drive us at our machines to the limit of endurance.

UNTIL—until we return again to Crisis!

For, so long as machinery is still perfected, we driven at still greater speed, our wages buying back ever less of the wealth that we create, a new and vaster surplus will pile up—a new and greater crisis will come upon us.

Death, starvation and misery often worse than death, will again stare the working class in the face. . . .

And again we will be driven to war. . . .

For war is the bloody antidote—the War-Dead are the Antibodies—to the cumulative poison in the body of Capitalism which threatens its life.

We are compelled to die in order that the Monster which threatens to destroy us may revive and live.

This then is the Law of Capitalism—inescapable under the system:

When we have labored and created vast stores of the food, shelter and clothing we need, we are compelled to suffer hunger and destitution in the midst of the plenty we have created. . . .

AND—

That we might not rise and take possession of our own, we are driven to war . . . to kill other workers and be killed by them . . . in order to help our bosses fasten new chains upon distant peoples, and so strengthen the old chains upon those of us who survive the slaughter. . . .

I looked with clearer eyes upon the world about me. The machine, destined to be the last slave in history, destined one day to free a classless world from care and want and insecurity, has become in the hands of an exploiting class in the course of a century, the iron Taskmaster of the million-folked peoples of the earth . . . a Robot Jailer of countless prisoners of Starvation. . . .

• • •

Will the tragic cycle recur without end?

"No," said the Socialist Party. "No. We will organize and educate the workers. We will capture one parliamentary position after another. And when we have a majority we will begin to transform the old order . . . by gradual stages. . . ."

Now and again we would meet a socialist who quarreled with this non-Marxian position of the Party: "Marx teaches us that one day Capitalism will be unable to overcome its crisis, then the workers will rise and seize power, and change the motives of industry from private profit to human use."

We were a decade distant from the Ten Days That Shook the World, and a quarter of a century from the collapse that is today shaking the capitalist world to its foundations. The World War was still seven years off; beside, only two years behind us lay the failure of the 1905 Russian Revolution. Later events would clear the fog for many an unclear socialist, but those events were still in the womb of History. In those days only a few in the party were Marxists; the rest of us were hardly aware of their existence. The Socialist Party was not then as it is not today a party of proletarian revolution. It was as it is a party of petit-bourgeois social reform; though it covered its character with revolutionary phrases. The few Marxists in the party were lost to the mass of reformism and confusion that characterized the ranks and the officialdom. The party's officialdom held the party press securely in its control. The outlook of most of us was limited by the limitations of the official organ.

I suffered confusion along with the rest. It appeared to me in those early years not impossible or improbable that the workers will be permitted by legal means, under capitalist law and government, to capture the machinery of the capitalist state, and within that state gradually transform capitalism into socialism. And so long as I suffered from that delusion I rejected the claim of the Marxian Socialists: that the collapse of Capitalism will come long before the Socialist Parties can "capture" capitalist parliaments; that in that collapse the workers will be forced to choose between starvation and revolution, and will be compelled to fight for their very existence—because no ruling class in history has ever surrendered its power without a violent struggle.

Thus in all my public work I maintained the Party position. "In a democracy (we have the right to expect) the ballot will prevail." At times an objector in the meeting would ask, "But what if the ballot should be knocked from our hands?" "Then," I would reply, "the people will have no other recourse save revolution." But though I recognized the possibility of revolution I had faith in the effectiveness of "democracy." "When a majority of the workers vote for socialism the will of the majority must prevail," I said.

This was more than a decade before Fascism appeared; Fascism—the open dictatorship of the bosses and the landlords; Fascism—"Bourgeois Democracy" with its gumshoe off, exposing the Iron Heel.

J.G. Phelps Stokes read much Socialist theory and he held the dominant party position. I, being a worker with no schooling, looked up to Graham in all matters theoretical: He "*knew*"; I was learning.

"The American Revolution" said Graham (full-page interview in *The New York Times*, October 23, 1910) "was an economic revolt—far more than a revolt for freedom of conscience—against private tax-gatherings by non-participants in labor. But the tax was but a pittance levied on a luxury—on tea. Today the whole American people are taxed, not tuppence a pound on a luxury, but on the necessities of life to an extent approximating one half of their entire product. If revolt, if armed and bloody revolt, was justified in 1776, it is infinitely more justified today, in view of the infinitely greater wrong that is done the people." But he added, "I do not advocate violent revolt at this time, or for the near future, for the reason that I firmly believe this situation can be remedied without it." How? "By means of the widest Socialistic propaganda, to the end that the common sense of the people themselves shall constitute such an insurmountable obstacle to the continuance of their exploitation, that the exploiters will permit continuing limitations of their opportunities, until unearned profit-taking shall no longer be a possibility."[3] It was a favorite theory with him that the gradual losses would be spread evenly over the capitalist class from its least to its most important member and so painlessly and unawaredly will they be put out of existence as a class that they will not even dream of resistance.

Thus I held with him that there would be time for, and that the capitalist class and its government would allow, a peaceful war of attrition in which the profits of the landlords and the bosses would be crowded out of existence! . . .

With this illusion, we both went about the country stating the case for socialism—against capitalism.

We were popular with many elements beside the working class: First, because of these very illusions: secondly, because "Mr. Stokes is a member of one of the most distinguished and aristocratic families in New York, and a descendant of several early Governors of New England"; and, thirdly, because he was, moreover "the 'hero' of 'our' greatest social romance, a figure in the one romance of recent years that has come nearer than any other to demonstrating the ideal of universal brotherhood."

Our political reformist position, Mr. Stokes's wealth and social position, and the romantic glamor with which our marriage was surrounded, brought us invitations from the most incredible sources: "Come tell us about Socialism." Daughters of the American Revolution (really Dames of the American Reaction) who pointed to us as proof that in "free" and "democratic" America any working girl can marry a millionaire; churches; various church societies; church congresses; church dinners, conferences; patriotic and traditional groups (The Grant Family, etc.), city, civic, reform, progressive, and liberal clubs; clubs of business men, of women; chautauquas; social service gatherings; school, settlements;—we talked Socialism nearly everywhere except in out-and-out Republican and Democratic Clubs, and Catholic, or Jewish Orthodox churches, though I am not sure that we were never invited!

There were Comrades who argued against our speaking before these non-working class organizations: "No use bringing the message of Socialism to its logical enemies," they said. "Besides, they are only curious about you, or they want the publicity you bring them." But experience taught me the value of accepting these invitations. Many came out of curiosity, but remained to listen, and that was important. Moreover, they often stayed to take sides. As a rule these bodies were controlled by wealthy bosses and landlords of the town—or their paid servants and retainers; but many workers and poor farmers, or people of the lower middle class, attended the meetings. The question our meetings raised—that of Socialism versus Capitalism—clarified the class struggle for those present; placed the exploiting elements on one side, the exploited on the other. This was clear in the questions asked, the objections raised, and in the heated after discussions.

We were not always invited with the expectation of giving an out-and-out Socialist talk. For years after we had joined the Socialist Party, the Capitalist press continued to refer to us as the "noted Settlement workers." Those inviting us often thought therefore, to sponsor a harmonizing, innocuous talk in which the facts of the class struggle would not appear. When they found us drawing class lines their consternation was undisguised. During the discussion, their frantic efforts to swing sentiment against socialism exposed their own class interest to the workers and farmers present. For these it was an unforgettable lesson in class antagonisms. As for us—their leaders would never again vote to put us on their programs! . . .

There were exceptions, of course. Notwithstanding our attacks upon their class privileges, there were those among them—the honored few—who would bravely approve our stand. But they were exceptions to an outstanding rule. A second invitation to address these organizations was rare. However, we filled first engagements (between meetings of workers) for a number of years, and covered very wide territory.

Oscar Wilde, a degenerate gentleman of the British aristocracy, remarked about Frank Harris—not so much a gentleman though possibly a little more degenerate, "Frank has been invited to all the great houses in London—once."

I might say without too great exaggeration (though first warning the reader to adjust the dreadful analogy), "We have been invited to speak before all the conservative organizations in America—once."

We frequently made very interesting contacts in these meetings, out of which grew extended friendships. I recall the engaging young professor I met in Chautauqua in 1913. He was from the University of Pennsylvania, and came to deliver a series of lectures on social and economic questions. He could not see his way clear to socialism. Many questions troubled him. So we sat on the long low porch of the main hotel and talked till the small hours of the morning.

I have a pencilled note before me, written by this young professor on his way home from Chautauqua the week following our talk. It reads:

7/25/1913

Erie train—Jamestown to Elmira

Dear lady,—you will be glad to hear of the real stirring-up that resulted from your talk last week. [Victor] Berger came after you and made an excellent speech, but none of the men who spoke—with all due respect to Mr. Stokes—got the grip on that crowd that you did. You disturbed them so that for days after you left they talked about your address. Some were pro and some were con, but very few were on the fence. You forced them to be either for you or against you. Better than that, you force both sides to think. Hundreds, perhaps thousands, who never took the matter seriously before are doing so now. It was a big piece of work.

That is why I wish that there were more people like you going up and down the world. It is a joy to see the effectiveness of your word. It is a source of profound satisfaction to see how mightily truth may prevail when it is well handled. Best of all, you find time in your pilgrimages to grasp some of us by the hand and call us Comrades.

Thank you, Comrade.

Scott Nearing.

It was not long before Scott Nearing joined the Socialist Party. Some years after he became a Socialist, he went further and by the logical pressure of events graduated into Communism.[4]

• • •

"Dear, only a little longer."

"You've stood here long enough."

"But there are still so many people, I can't leave them."

"They'll stay as long as we do, and you'll drop if I don't take you away."

"But I'm not a bit tired."

"I'm exhausted."

A glance at his face, and I would try to tear myself away from the life-giving touch of their hands.

Night after night, in those early years, the same struggle. At the ends of meetings workers pressing forward for a handclasp and a word. . . . To me the experience was like healing, after the wearying rail journeys, after the feverish agony before speeches. I loved their faces—the faces of my own—of toilworn men, of careworn women—of pale children who would live to see the Dawn of a New Day. I could not get close enough to them when the speeches were done. Indeed, if the platform was high, and far removed from the first rows, giving me a sense of distance from my audience I spoke with great effort; but when I found myself on a low platform, the chairs almost touching it, the workers almost breathing into my face, I spoke with great ease and fluency. No, I could not get close enough to them. The speeches done, the questions and discussion ended, I was filled again with new life and energy when the crowd pressed forward and I could touch hands with my class.

To look into their eyes where shone the hope of a new future, to press their hands that would take power and hold it for the freedom of the human race, to speak a word more—to each—"Remember: Organize, organize!"—to hear them tell me of their own experiences—experiences that burnt anew in me the lesson of the workers' struggles—why, at the end I would always say: "Now I could start the evening all over again, I feel so renewed."

But Graham always wearied. I could not understand how it was with him. "Come on, Girlie, I am tired to death!" he would moan, "Let's get out of this, come!" . . .

After the meeting, when we were alone in the home of some comrade or in a hotel room, Graham would expostulate: "But where is the sense?

Do try to cut those after-meetings short. Let's get away from the hall as soon as the meetings are over. I can't stand those handshakings; they exhaust me beyond words. . . ."

Strange! . . .

It was not until many years afterward that I realized why this was so with him. Then it was borne in on me that he loved the people *in theory only*; that there was no personal warmth in him for them. Often I thought I detected a look of contempt for some member or members of my class. He could not have dealt me a personal blow that would have hurt more. At times he would let fall a word . . . and I would chill with an undefined apprehension.

By 1909–1910 Graham was making occasional speeches only. And it was not long before he had shut himself away in his study. He would devote himself to writing; he would write a book to prove the (bourgeois) economic motive in the formation of the American Government. He spent days, weeks, months in the American History Room of the Public Library, and, practically all the rest of his time outside it, in his private study; reading, making notations, cataloging his material.

It will be a much-needed work, I thought; and grew enthusiastic. In my spare time between strikes and mass meetings and at the end of tours, I worked eagerly with him; dug for material in the American History Room, copied it on cards for his card-case.

After he had been several years on his notes, I think, Professor Beard's book on the "Economic Interpretation of the United States Constitution" appeared. Graham came to me and announced the fact of its publication without the slightest regret, or sign of feeling for the time and effort he had given the work that was now superfluous. On the contrary, there was relief in his tone as he observed: "it would now be senseless to continue with the work. I would only be duplicating what Professor Beard has done so admirably. . . ." In fact, the writing had not been begun. It was still in the stage of notes and files and catalogs. . . .

"Maybe now we can go on tour *together* again, for the Party," I suggested hopefully.

"No, Girlie, I'm tired of running around the country, making speeches," he said.

And I, still unsuspecting, awaited the time when he would recover from his strange weariness.

• • •

My name came to be prominently associated with strikes and mass movements. Respectable bourgeois organizations no longer considered me desirable. Even first invitations were no longer unanimous. I recall with a twinkle the stubborn fight put up by the Reverend Paul Revere Frothingham, Pastor of the richest Unitarian Church in America, the Arlington Street Church in Boston's aristocratic Back Bay. For three years the Unitarian Fellowship for Social Justice had been opening its Anniversary Week in the Arlington Street Church. This year—1913— the Fellowship was again to open its program in that exclusive edifice, but had planned its program without consulting the Reverend Paul Revere Frothingham! A week before the opening night the reverend gentleman discovered that two women radicals were scheduled to speak. Beside my talk on Socialism, the beautiful and gifted Inez Milholland— she of the revolutionary spirit—was to make a plea for equal suffrage.[5] The Reverend Paul Revere Frothingham would not have it. No radicalism shall desecrate his pulpit—especially, the press reported, on a Sunday night!

However, the Unitarian Fellowship for Social Justice insisted that they would nevertheless carry out their program. The agitation in Boston and its Back Bay became so intense that for an entire week the fight raged on the front page of Boston's dailies, while mildly alarmed editorials appeared in papers far from Boston to point a lesson: This is not the way to bring the vanishing masses back into the churches! . . . Nevertheless, when the time came for opening the program (May 18) the Reverend Paul Revere Frothingham, influenced by the "upper" classes, not by the masses, clung to his pulpit. Whereupon, the Unitarian Fellowship hired a hall!

The exodus from the Arlington Street Church was led by a courageous young minister, the Reverend John Haynes Holmes, who later was driven out of the church. And while the Reverend Frothingham held on to his pulpit, I addressed an immense gathering at the opening session in Ford Hall. And not alone was Ford Hall filled to overflowing, but there was an overflow meeting in a hall around the corner. From there too, the Reverend Albert Rhys Williams (whom I later called Comrade, and who, after the Russian Proletarian Revolution helped to organize the Red Army) invited me to speak in the Maverick Church of which he was pastor.[6] I occupied his pulpit and talked socialism to eleven hundred people who crowded the barnlike structure. The opposition of the Reverend Paul Revere Frothingham merely helped to bring three audiences where one would normally have been expected.

In fact, the meetings were more than three: The Reverend Albert Rhys Williams gave me several later opportunities to speak from his pulpit; while the Arlington Street episode was followed by what is commonly called an "act of poetic justice." On November fifth of that year— less than five months after my exclusion from the Paul Revere Frothingham pulpit, I received a cordial invitation from the Unitarian Society of Newton Centre, Massachusetts, Alson H. Robinson, Minister, to address his congregation. Part of his letter read:

"Last Sunday afternoon I placed this entire matter [of a Forum for the discussion of social problems] before the Executive Committee of my Church, in an appeal to use the building for the proposed series of meetings. I pictured to them as graphically as I was able the awful consequences which might be expected to result from the appearance of such a person as yourself at one of these weekly meetings. You can imagine my great delight at the unanimous vote in favor of giving me the use of the Church without any strings attached to it."

And my own peculiar delight can be imagined when I read what followed:

"In connection with your exclusion from the Arlington Street Church last spring," wrote Mr. Robinson, "you may be interested to learn that the pulpit formerly used in that Church is now performing very humble service in my Church here in Newton Centre . . . And I am sure if you will do it the honor of accepting its hospitality you will feel quite at home."

I did—once. As usual, there was no second invitation. But—as usual—I considered the lost opportunity well worth while.

In 1906, Jack London spoke at Yale University and made an out-and-out revolutionary talk. He spoke under the auspices of the Intercollegiate Socialist Society which was organized "to promote an intelligent interest in the subject of socialism among college men and women."

This speech was a signal for violent attacks upon socialism by the Paul Revere Frothinghams in the field of education. The storm raised at Yale was felt over a wide field.[7] And since not all college students are rich men's sons and daughters, the ferment worked admirably. The students began to take a live interest in the subject, and the young Intercollegiate Socialist Society, was definitely put "on the map." By 1913 the I.S.S. had organized between sixty and seventy Chapters in as many American colleges and universities, and more than a dozen alumni Chapters. J.G. Phelps Stokes, Helen Phelps Stokes, Mary Sanford, William English Walling, John Spargo, Upton Sinclair, and many other well-known socialists of the period were active in the I.S.S. as lecturers, or executive members; or writers for its Quarterly, *The Intercollegiate Socialist.*

For a number of years, between mass meetings and strike activities, I toured the country for the I.S.S. In that time I covered scores of colleges and universities, and learned that the big bosses by their support controlled the country's educational institutions as they controlled the press, and all other avenues for moulding sentiment.

One of my earliest lessons in this field was prior to 1910, when Chancellor Day fought bitterly against my speaking at Syracuse University.[8] Chancellor Day was a friend of John D. Rockefeller who was a "friend" of the institution. We had met the Chancellor not so long before at a Baptist dinner in the old Astor House. We had been invited to address this gathering on the subject of the Social Settlement. The invitation came at a time when Graham and I were contemplating a public repudiation of the social settlement movement as one of reaction, of subtle corruption of the workers' minds, and as a stumbling-block to their own class organization. We decided to accept the invitation and at the Dinner announce our repudiation of the settlements and give our reasons therefor.

At the speakers' table was Chancellor Day, large and imposing. We also faced a Mr. Archibald [sic]—a quiet little man with a pleasing countenance, a keen gray-blue eye and—I imagined, a keen ear for all the talk.[9] We learned that he was an associate of Mr. Rockefeller in his oil business. There was much glorious oratory but Graham's talk and mine created consternation. Chancellor Day took up the cudgels for the social settlements, and for days afterward the controversy raged on the front pages of some of the metropolitan dailies whence it was carried far beyond the limits of the metropolitan area. Chancellor Day soon thereafter, and for the same reason that he defended the settlements, took violent exception to my speaking at Syracuse. His opposition stirred great interest. The meeting was held in a very large hall of the university. The hall was crowded to the very doors with students, members of the Faculty, and friends of both; most of whom the Chancellor helped to bring. And at the meeting we discussed the question not only of Socialism but of who controls Syracuse University. I learned thereafter to look for—and rarely failed to find—the source of such opposition in some rich man's support of the institution.

At times a study group was compelled to hire a hall. But, as in the case of the Unitarian Fellowship, Socialism was always the gainer. The authorities of Cincinnati's own college, for example, by their opposition (1913) provided us with a crowded hall outside the college.[10] Our meeting opened the new auditorium of the Woman's City Club. Five or six hundred students, townspeople and members of the Faculty came to hear the talk. So inspired was the gathering that I forgot my temperature of 102.6 (my chronic bronchitis again!) and carried the meeting for over three hours—collapsing only after it was well over, when a Mr. and Mrs. Max Senior, wholly sympathetic and concerned, took me in charge.

At the University of Rochester the Chairman of the Board of Trustees was said to have exclaimed in a Board meeting on the eve of my scheduled talk [March 1914]: "Gentlemen, I stand second to none in my efforts to uphold the principle of freedom of speech, but there is a limit to expression!" I spoke to a large gathering of students and faculty members who refused to support the slogan: "Think what you please, but don't say anything."

In the scores of colleges and universities where I addressed student groups, classes, mixed meetings of students and townsfolk or entire student bodies in "chapel," I had many friendly receptions as well. Princeton's President, the President of Hobart, and heads of other universities entertained me in their own homes when I came to speak at their institutions. But I realized that they were merely seeking to honor the highly respectable family into which I had married and not the message I had come to bring. Institutions which depended for their support upon wealthy men, big exploiters of labor, can hardly afford to welcome a message which exposes the sources of their robbery. Ordinarily there was opposition, and opposition usually meant stimulated interest and good meetings.

Always the interest among the worker-students and the poorly-paid instructors and professors was keen. It was these who gave me the widest hearing. It was to these that we came with our message.

The student who was working his way—or whose parents or entire family were working his way—through college was the student to reach.

Boys and girls from poor workers' or farmers' homes or from the lower-middle class were getting their muscles crammed with sports, and their minds with "culture" from books on the Five-Foot Shelf. One day their brains would be thrown upon the labor market—white-collar commodities, to be bought up cheap by capitalism. Rationalization would make thousands of these superfluous to their employers as tens of thousands of workers in other fields were becoming. It was my task to persuade these students to discard the concepts represented in the Five-Foot concoction of Charles William Eliot, Emeritus of Harvard University, glorifier of the scab and advocate of strike-breaking, and turn to the Five-Foot Shelf of Marxian Theory. And whenever a student joined the Socialist Study Chapter, or when I succeeded in organizing a Chapter where none had been before, I was happy; for I felt that those who sell their labor power above the collar-line, and those who sell their labor power below the cuff-line are class brothers—equally insecure, equally exploited, equally enslaved under Capitalism.

The last of my tours for the Intercollegiate Socialist Society was made to "break new ground" in the southern states: Maryland, Virginia, District of Columbia, the Carolinas, Georgia etc. I find a letter dated Columbia, South Carolina, December 14, 1916, written by Professor [Josiah] Morse to the I.S.S. which gives in some detail my visit to Columbia. It is typical of the eagerness with which the message was listened to at Chapel Hill, North Carolina and other college and university centers in the South:

> . . . Mrs. Stokes . . . arrived Friday noon and at night christened our new High School Auditorium with a lecture on equal suffrage before a large and representative audience. It was certainly a new and very interesting kind of talk on the subject. Socialism fairly oozed out of every sentence. There was considerable discussion, for this part of the country, after the lecture. Saturday afternoon, she spoke in the same auditorium on Socialism straight. This was under the auspices of the university Chapter of the I.S.S., and after the lecture there was a large reception in her honor. Sunday she spoke on Prohibition in a theatre to a large audience. I venture to say that never before had such a large audience such a lecture on Prohibition. With Prohibition for a background she painted . . . the evils of Capitalism and the remedies offered by Socialism. Monday morning she spoke in the University Chapel to the entire student body, giving them in a nutshell the essence of Socialism, and impressing upon them the importance of studying it. Next she was taken by a group of colored people to one of their churches. From there she was hurried to Benedict College (colored) where she spoke several times and made an impression those stu-

dents will not soon forget. At four, she lectured in one of the University Halls again, followed by considerable discussion, and at seven she attended a luncheon given by the social workers of the city, speaking from half past eight to half past ten! Quite a strenuous day even for a Socialist . . . She was the "talk of the town" and folks were discussing Socialism who before her arrival did not know whether it was a new disease like Infantile Paralysis, or some new breakfast food . . .

At the same time I wrote the I.S.S.:

Dr. Morse says that I have done an "impolitic" thing, and that it might have resulted very badly for the U. of S.C. Chapter if the matter had got into the papers—a "calamity" which was "averted" by telephoning to "headquarters" in time. The facts are these: Morse asked if I would speak at Benedict College. It surprised me to learn that there was a college at Columbia which had not been included in my itinerary. "Colored," he explained. This made no difference in the world to me. I went and spoke, and found the students alert, intelligent, responsive. And since the president—a Dr. Valentine—did not object, I proceeded to organize a Chapter (27 members!).[11] When I returned and conveyed the glad news to Morse he was in despair: If it were to be known anywhere in the Southern colleges that Negro chapters had been organized it would kill all effort and interest. I argued that possibly the young Southern Gentlemen might be reconciled to the study of Socialism even if black students were studying the subject too. No, Dr. Morse argued, it would mean more than that—it would mean belonging to a Society that held conventions and met through delegations; and meeting a Negro on terms of social equality was *unthinkable*. Said he, should the I.S.S. place Benedict College on its letterhead it would be the end of all effort. I was appalled at this attitude. It is difficult for me to understand the feeling that exists. Of course, having been advised to speak there I naturally took the opportunity to organize too. William McKinley Scott will be secretary of the 27. Won't you send him the study course, please?

Fraternally,
R.P.S.

The I.S.S. was very careful to keep the Negro and white student groups segregated in the South. The Society, today the League for Industrial Democracy, has moved steadily with the Socialist Party, its parent organization, into a position of white chauvinism and—in line with its general counter-revolutionary policy, it Jim-Crows its Negro students in the colleges as the Socialist Party helps to Jim-Crow the Negro workers in the reactionary A.F. of L. unions.

CHAPTER V

War

In the spring of 1914 I visited England with my friend, Olive Tilford Dargan (Fielding Burke).

Hadley, Hertfordshire, was a short bus ride from London. In Hadley Wood we read, and wrote, and took long tramps over hill and dale of the lovely countryside. Here I discovered that the year had five seasons: Spring, Summer, Autumn, Winter, and English Spring—the last the sweetest season of them all! But Nature's loveliness here, as elsewhere in the capitalist world, was dimmed by human misery and insecurity. The song, which I began joyously, praising the pearly hedgerows, the notes of the robin, the blackbird, the lark heard for the first time and not known or discovered till its thrilling outburst was spent, had to end with deeper realities for the human heart:

> The hour grew late—and I began
> To carol to the homeward track
> But when I turned I saw a man—
> A man with bundle on his back;
> A beggar's bundle on his back
> And in his eye was England's ban . . .
> Oh, England!

Often we would leave Hadley Wood for London, to take part in mass

meetings, to mingle with the demonstrators in the Equal Suffrage movement or attend a lecture at Albert Hall.

One day we visited Puma Court—the Red Lion court of my childhood. The women gathered about us and told us of a "Little girl who
lived here years ago; then went to America, grew up, and married a
fine gentleman—a millionaire . . . And didn't they come right here to
London to visit us—right up to this very court! And we were ready with
a fine committee and a real celebration and all. But would you believe
it—when she got here—right over there, at that end of the court—
with her fine husband and her grand car and her chauffeur, she was suddenly ashamed to show him where she had lived once in poverty among
her poor neighbors. She turned right around, drove off in her grand
automobile. I tell you it gave us a turn to have her ashamed to introduce
him to us!"

"But maybe . . ."

I did not tell them that I was the little girl they knew.

I returned to America shortly before the fateful August First. War was
to break out within a few short weeks, but of war and the nearness of
war I was wholly unaware.

◆ ◆ ◆

With the outbreak of war there was much ferment in the Socialist
Party. What it was about I did not know or inquire. For years I had gone
about the country stirring interest in Socialism. I had thrown myself
into strikes with the fury of a true soldier in the ranks of my class. Nothing was too difficult; all-night picketings, all-day activity, at times no
sleep, no food; it did not matter. Often I kept going until I broke, and
had to be dragged away from the scene of battle. There came no call
of any kind to aid in the struggle to which I did not respond with joy.
Another blow at the enemy, another and another! But when it came
to the question of inner party struggles, I said: "I'm too busy fighting
the common enemy—Capitalism. I have no time or effort to spare for
fighting my comrades." Or: "Let those who want to get into Party fights,
do so. They know. I leave these questions to them." I did not run away

from the inner-party struggles. I simply found no time for them, and did not realize their importance. That was my misfortune. I lacked clarification on that account. Had I taken part in these struggles I would never have left the Party with Spargo, Walling, Russell, and Graham. Graham would have gone as he went, no doubt; but not I. I would have gone later with the Left Wing (as I did, after rejoining in 1918), but not earlier, with the social-patriot Right.

Between tours, at Caritas, I was constantly surrounded by those Party members who later went over to the camp of Reaction. It was inevitable that I should resign from the Party with them.

It was my misfortune to suffer the confusions spread by this group of secessionists: "Before war broke there was some sense in opposing it. But not now. It is not our business now as Socialists to cry Peace, Peace! Yes, I reasoned; it is our business to go among the people explaining how and why Capitalism is the cause of war, and to exhort the workers to do away with the system that breeds war. Otherwise, I reasoned, we do as the preachers do, who inveigh against poverty, hunger and misery without striking at their cause—Capitalism; without joining in the fight to abolish Capitalism." Graham brought me a paper—I signed, resigning with the group from the party. My position was the Guesdeist position: Militarism is an effect of Capitalism.[1] Why scold effects? Strike at the cause! Don't strike at war but at the system which breeds war. . . . I was wrong in principle. Capitalism breeds war, and Capitalist governments declare war, but workers and farmers wage war. It is not in the interest of the workers to fight their masters' wars. Imperialist wars are conducted to further enslave workers and enrich bosses. There can be but one war for workers—a war to end Capitalism; to end slavery. But of this for the time being I had lost sight. Without being aware, I forsook principle; forsook the interests of my class; forsook, through their interests, the future interest of all mankind.

This in 1916! Not so long before, Helen Keller, one of the most remarkable women in America, the blind deaf-mute who had learned to speak with a voice she could not hear, to audiences she could not see, spoke as follows to workers who crowded the auditorium of the Washington Irving High School:

> The useless burden of war always falls heaviest upon the mass of the people. It kills vast numbers of men who build, dig, reap, plough and feed the world. They do not know why they are sent to die. They suffer for all the miseries of war while their rulers reap all of the rewards. Their wages have not been raised, their toil made lighter, or their homes more decent. When they can no longer bear the misery caused by small pay, long hours and uncertain employment, they go on strike. Then the patriotic capitalists send the militia and even troops to crush them. And on top of that they are asked to join the militia and the army to fight for liberty they have never known. Schools and all sorts of organizations are turned to the purposes of the war makers. Let no workingman join the army that is organized by order of Congress. As President Wilson has pointed out in his message, that army will defend the interests of the capitalists. It is an army that can be used to break strikes as well as to defend the people. You do not want that kind of preparedness, do you? If the democratic measures of preparedness fall before the advance of world empire, the workingman has nothing to fear. No conqueror will beat down his wages and wreck his unions more ruthlessly than his own fellow citizens of the capitalist class are doing. Nor will a union of the capitalist class of the world be able to oppress him more than the masters of his own country have done. The worker has nothing to lose but his chains and he has a world to win. He can win it all at once from a world empire. Let them call us traitor and baptize our international association with fire and steel. It shall court death rather than surrender to ruinous patriotism. There is a place in the world today for a defiant union of all workers to destroy the war of the trenches and to end the paying of tribute by the workers of the world.[2]

The occasion was a peace meeting; and I was chairman of the meeting. Yet soon thereafter I had lost the true outlook. I was a member of the Women's Peace Party, of other pacifist organizations. This, in the first flush of opposition to the war. But I was not content with pacifism. I did not know what was wrong with the position, but I soon found myself disagreeing with it, quarreling with it inwardly. No, the cry of peace, peace could not destroy the war of the trenches. But what could? I did not know. There was no program of action against war of which I was aware. The working-class struggle was not politically matured. The Russian Proletarian revolution had not yet become an historic fact. There was as yet no Communist International—symbol of the maturing struggle, to cry to the workers of all lands: "Answer the bosses war with war upon your own Capitalist warmakers!" I did not see anything definite—any active program to reach out for.

When Henry Ford wired me:

> Will you come as my guest on board the Oscar II of the Scandinavian-American Line, sailing from New York December fourth for Christiana, Stockholm and Copenhagen.

and added:

> I am cabling men and women of the European nations to join us enroute and at some central point to be determined later to establish an international conference dedicated to negotiations leading to a just settlement of the war. A hundred representative Americans are being invited.

and argued:

> With twenty thousand men killed every twenty-four hours, tens of thousands maimed, homes ruined, another winter begun, the time has come for a few men and women with courage and energy irrespective of the cost in personal inconvenience, money sacrificed, and criticism to free the good will of Europe that it may assert itself for peace and justice with the strong probability that international disarmament can be accomplished.

I immediately replied:

> If I felt you saw eye to eye with me . . . I would gladly join you . . . but I feel that you stand for and foster the very conditions that have caused this war—conditions, which, if fostered further, will make for future wars . . .

And because the Capitalists, not the people, are in control, nothing other than a complete test of arms will be allowed to settle the question. Doctors widely disagreeing on the diagnosis and consequently upon the course of treatment, should not together attend the patient. . . . I regard your diagnosis as wrong and your proposed treatment as futile. . . . Therefore, much as I desire "peace by Christmas" and the establishment of permanent peace in the future . . . I must . . . decline your exceedingly kind invitation.[3]

Yes, I wanted peace but came blindly to stand for the war. It was a war for markets, yet I began to see it wrongly as a war for democracy. It was a war of European and American Capitalism for control of oil in the East. I came to see it distortedly as something beside—as a war of liberation—a war that would precipitate the Social Revolution! For was not every Socialist I knew looking for it—in Germany? To defeat the German Kaiser and German Imperialism, then, came to be the same thing in my mind with the victory of the working-class revolution. I began to feel grateful to Woodrow Wilson for all his fine words about "war for democracy." When Wilson spoke of the "people," I failed to see that he had in mind the bourgeois supporters of Capitalism, not the toiling masses, not the enslaved workers of field and factory. I said, Wilson has vision, Wilson sees. As if any representative of Capitalism ever can see the real needs of the working class, least of all labor in their interest. I was grateful. I was grateful to the American soldiers as I watched them march away to fight for world "democracy." I began to see America under Wilson as a new kind of America—as a cultural America placing itself at the service of the people, the masses. Blind! I was blind!

Graham and I were out of the Party. But we felt in no way out of Socialism. Or, should I speak only for myself? One day, Graham came to me with a whispered confidence: "Samuel Gompers is moving closer to Socialism, and can be got to take a Socialist position." The American League for Labor and Democracy was to be organized as a "bridge" to make "the passing over of Gompers into the Socialist Camp" easier for him. . . . Graham knows about such things. I do not. . . . I had confidence in his word. "We must join the League," he said. Of course, we must join the League. Leftward Ho! The A.F. of L. was moving Left, and would soon be a genuinely working-class organization! Chimerical! As chimerical as that Wilson would embrace a democracy to include the great majority of the people—the toiling masses! As chimerical as that the defeat of the Kaiser and the rise of the German Social-Democracy would bring the German working class revolution; would bring, and not retard it for more than a decade; would bring, and not drown it in the blood of thousands of the bravest and best fighters on the forefront of the working-class struggle, including the blood of Rosa Luxemburg and Karl Liebknecht! . . . [4]

◆ ◆ ◆

I soon found myself surrounded by motley political elements. Can these be the friends of the working class? Reactionary A.F. of L. officials, bourgeois reformers; birth control advocates who offered birth control not for what it was—a cause well worth fighting for, but as a panacea for all the evils of wage slavery; liberal dinner clubbers—petit-bourgeois anarchists; government officials. . . .

Mr. Jacobs of the old Cigar Makers Union Local No. 13 looked me up. I must go with him to one of the big factories and "make a few." At the bench: "Just a little newsreel please!" So, the "people" of the petit-bourgeois world were suddenly proud of me! Ancient reactionary acquaintances began to look me up. A Madam B. wrote a scenario— "The Least-Loved Rich Woman in the World" in "Sacred Motherhood" etc. etc. Her company would give me the leading role. The manager of C.K.Y. [actress Clara Kimball Young] made a reel of me, declared me a Sarah Bernhardt and offered me a contract. Wealthy townswomen drew me into their homes through my interest in music or drama. . . . Ah, the President's daughter! A very charming young woman. I am delighted to meet Miss Margaret Wilson, quite on her own account. Will I not come and dine with her and her father—at the White House? Just a quiet, family dinner . . . The White House! A sudden wariness fills me. The White House after all—the seat of Capitalist power! What is wrong with me that I elicit such an invitation? The new contacts make me suspicious of myself. What is the matter? Old associates try to draw me into charity work, philanthropic, social. Back, back to the saccharine ancient darknesses! The paths that, in the interest of my class, I had long since forsaken—forsaken almost as quickly as I entered them! How can they believe that I would follow them again?

The National Party was formed in Chicago.[5] Suffice it to say, there was a shining list of names; Prohibitionists, Single Taxers, reactionary labor "leaders," well known liberals, progressives, eggressives (from the Socialist Party) and an unofficial observer from the White House . . . An imposing company—a labor party with labor left out.

Widespread reports of my connection with the National Party brought me messages of high approval and praise from many suspicious sources. To these I reacted with sharp self-criticism. Some, like the following, struck me with peculiar force:

Dear Mrs. Stokes:

Congratulations on your emancipation from party-slavery, and in your strong stand against the Teutonizing of Socialism.

I am eagerly awaiting the formation of an American Socialism that will recognize the principle of Nationalism. Thus will my quarrel with the party end, and I will ask that I be enrolled.

May I soon have the privilege of congratulating you on another forward step. I am opposed to parties in Zionism, but it would rejoice me if you joined the Poale-Zion, our socialist wing. This is your place, my friend, and you are sufficiently Jewish—nationally Jewish—to take your place in its ranks.

You know, of course, that Mary Antin is with us. But there is room for you. Come in.

A.H.F. (A.H. Fromenson)

Voices of the past, of darkness, of reaction! What has the Jewish worker in common with the Jewish exploiter? . . . Ah, Mr. Brudno! I embrace you, brother! Let us together make a home for ourselves in

Zion, yes? Or, here in America, you, the Jewish exploiter, I, your Jewish sweatshop slave! For are we not both united in Jewry?

The "principle of nationality"! Aye, back to sleep, worker! Forget your agonies, forget the class struggle, forget all that you have learned through the years, forget those that drain your blood and fatten on your toil. You are "patriots"—both of you—exploiter and slave, no? Both eager to stand by the scheme of things that enriches him, and starves you and yours. . . .

Workers, beware! The chauvinist embrace crushes you, you only. Him—the boss, the landlord, the capitalist politician, it leaves blood-stained victor—in full possession of the force and the freedom to devour you.

And when Baroness Halkett, Graham's oldest sister Sarah wrote me a social note; and added in the way of an unsupported by-the-bye: "I have followed the doings of the labor party with much interest. The *new* party of Socialists and Labor, I mean." I sat and fingered the note with the definite sensation of having been stung by a serpent.

A "labor" party in which *she* takes a friendly interest! I look long at the note. Sit at my desk and muse on her words. Then I write on the margin: "Note, what is the matter with my stand that Sarah can talk approvingly of it?"

Of Graham's eight brothers and sisters, Sarah Halkett is the least inclined to have any fellow feeling for labor. Harold, the youngest, is conservative but "tolerant." Mildred looks to her comfortable nest, and is not much concerned with politics. Ethel, mistress of millions, mother of an ample family, holds that "philanthropy" and "faith" will conquer all evil. Anson, secretary of Yale University and a minister of the church, is a forthright pillar of "Our Government"; he believes religion, education, and law and order, to be the answer to all problems. Helen, close and dear to me, had years back joined the Socialist Party. Caroline, in love with Bob Hunter,[6] her socialist husband, is content to leave the world of struggle to others. Newton, architect, ultra-conservative, monosyllabic—hard to say what he thinks or feels. But Sarah—Sarah had played with Liberal politics in England. David Lloyd George was an intimate friend, and had been a frequent guest at her home. She had learned all the Liberal Party's tricks of defeating the efforts of the worker to fight his own class battles, to win his own class ground. She feels not only an instinctive hatred for the militant class-conscious worker but is always actively interested in means to defeat him. Because of this, we are like fire and water; when we meet in the family drawing-room, or at the family dinner table, we bristle. And "Sadie" now expresses an interest in the "new" party of Socialists and Labor! . . .

The "interest" of these foes, more than the expressed concern of my friends, caused me to examine with deepening suspicion the path I was treading. The National Party was the still-born forerunner of fascism, built consciously by renegades from Socialism to cross over into the camp of reaction.

"Where is labor in this party?" Graham and John Spargo had no answer. They were "charming gentlemen" all, pleasant to meet in committee but gentlemen, no matter how great their charm, cannot build a party of the working class. I tendered my resignation.

Notes

INTRODUCTION

1. Arthur and Pearl Zipser, *Fire and Grace: The Life of Rose Pastor Stokes* (Athens & London: University of Georgia Press, 1990).

2. Quoted in Pat Creech Scholten, "Militant Women for Economic Justice: The Persuasion of Mary Harris Jones, Ella Reeve Bloor, Rose Pastor Stokes, Rose Schneiderman and Elizabeth Gurley Flynn," Ph.D. dissertation, Indiana University, 1978.

3. June Sochen, *Herstory: A Woman's View of American History* (New York: Alfred Publishing, 1974), 295. Rose Pastor Stokes wrote to Maxim Lieber regarding the women's movement: "I have sympathized with the movement only because I felt that the working woman was far backward in status and her political emancipation would help her to clearer consciousness of her place in the social economic world." She explained that she had earlier accepted male leadership "not from the point of their masculinity, but wholly from the point of view of their superior opportunities." Rose Pastor Stokes to Maxim Lieber, April 17, 1933, Rose Pastor Stokes Papers, Tamiment Library, New York University.

4. For an introduction to the work culture of early twentieth-century cigar workers, see Patricia A. Cooper, *Once a Cigar Maker: Men, Women and Work Culture in American Cigar Factories, 1900–1919* (Urbana and Chicago: University of Illinois Press, 1987). Regarding "buckeyes," Cooper writes that these were the "smallest units of production . . . which generally consisted of a lone

cigar maker operating his own shop, although some included one or two jour-
neymen" (81). Also see James O. Morris, *Conflict within the AFL: A Study of
Craft Versus Industrial Unionism, 1901–1938* (Ithaca: Cornell University Press,
1958). A sharply critical view of Gompers is to be found in Bernard Mandel,
Samuel Gompers: A Biography (Yellow Springs, Ohio: Antioch Press, 1963).

5. *Jewish Daily News,* July 22, 1901.

6. *Jewish Daily News,* March 23, 24, 1903.

7. *Jewish Daily News,* October 9, 1901.

8. *Jewish Daily News,* March 24, 1903.

9. *Jewish Daily News,* November 3, 1901; September 12, 26, 1901; October 1,
1901; November 14, 1902; October 25, 1903.

10. *Jewish Daily News,* October 15, 23, 1902; May 29, 1903.

11. "Next Year in Jerusalem," *Jewish Daily News*; "Kishineffing It," *Jewish
Daily News,* June 9, 1903.

12. *Jewish Daily News,* December 7, 1903.

13. Allen F. Davis, *Spearheads for Reform: The Social Settlements and the Progressive Movement, 1890–1914* (New York: Oxford University Press, 1967), 28.

14. Rose Harriet Pastor, "The Views of a Settlement Worker: A Talk with
J. G. Phelps Stokes," *Jewish Daily News* (ca. June–July 1903), clipping in Rose
Pastor Stokes Papers, Manuscripts and Archives, Yale University Library.

15. J. G. Phelps Stokes, "Public Schools as Social Centres," *The Annals of
the American Academy of Political and Social Science* 23 (1904): 457–63.

16. Rose H. Phelps Stokes, "The Condition of Working Women, from the
Working Woman's Viewpoint," *The Annals of the American Academy of Political
and Social Science* 27 (1906): 627–37.

17. *New York Times,* June 5, 1905.

18. Ibid.

19. The Municipal Ownership League, originally led by reformer Judge
Samuel Seabury, came under Hearst's control as a result of merger with the
William Randolph Hearst League. See W. A. Swanberg, *Citizen Hearst* (New
York: Scribners, 1961), 230–38.

20. Davis, *Spearheads for Reform,* 20–22.

21. Rockwell Kent, *It's Me, O Lord* (New York: Dodd, Mead, 1955), 187,
193–95.

22. Edward Marshall, "A Talk With the Richest Socialist in America," *New*

York Times, October 23, 1910.

23. *New York Times,* January 2, 1910.

24. See Matthew Josephson, *Union House-Union Bar* (New York: Random House, 1956), 96–99; also Kathleen Ann Sharp, "Rose Pastor Stokes: Radical Champion of the American Working Class, 1879–1933," Ph.D. dissertation, Duke University, 1979, pp. 84–88.

25. W. E. D. Stokes to Rose Pastor Stokes, June 24, 1912, Rose Pastor Stokes Papers, Tamiment Library, New York University.

26. The poem was published in the *Hoboken Socialist,* December 27, 1913.

27. Linda Gordon, *Woman's Body, Woman's Right: A Social History of Birth Control in America* (New York: Grossman, 1976), 226.

28. Margaret Sanger, *An Autobiography* (New York: Norton, 1938), 187–89.

29. Text of May 5, 1916, Carnegie Hall speech, Rose Pastor Stokes Papers, Manuscripts and Archives, Yale University Library.

30. *New York Times,* May 6, 1916.

31. Jessie Ashley, quoted in Gordon, *Woman's Body, Woman's Right,* 232.

32. Anson Phelps Stokes to Rose Pastor Stokes, May 21, 1916, and Rose Pastor Stokes to Anson Phelps Stokes, May 29, 1916, Rose Pastor Stokes Papers, Manuscripts and Archives, Yale University Library.

33. See Rose Pastor Stokes, *The Woman Who Wouldn't* (New York and London: Putnam's, 1916).

34. Rose Pastor Stokes to Emily Greene Balch, December 28, 1916, Rose Pastor Stokes Papers, Yale University Library; also Emily Greene Balch to Rose Pastor Stokes, December 27, 1916, Rose Pastor Stokes Papers, Tamiment Library, New York University. On March 17, 1917, Stokes resigned from the Woman's Peace Party, writing: "If the United States were to become involved in the war I would place myself at the service of the country. . . . This great war, by the iron necessities of its efficient conduct, is compelling the creation of newer more unifying institutions (even against the powerful selfish interests within each nation)." Her thought here was in keeping with that of many of the progressive intellectuals. See Rose Pastor Stokes to the chairman and executive committee of the Woman's Peace Party of New York, March 17, 1917, Rose Pastor Stokes Papers, Tamiment Library, New York University.

35. See list of contributing members of the Vigilantes, August 1917, Rose Pastor Stokes Papers, Manuscripts and Archives, Yale University Library.

36. See *New York Times*, May 13, 1917; also see account in the *Baltimore Sun*, May 13, 1917.

37. Rose Pastor Stokes, "A Confession," *Century* (December 1917): 457–59.

38. For an account of the National party see Kenneth E. Hendrickson, Jr., "The Pro-War Socialists, the Social Democratic League and the Ill-Fated Drive for Industrial Democracy in America, 1917–1920," *Labor History* (Summer 1970): 304–322.

39. Rose Pastor Stokes to Eph. Karelsen, December 17, 1917, Rose Pastor Stokes Papers, Manuscripts and Archives, Yale University Library.

40. See Richard L. Watson, Jr., *The Development of National Power* (Washington: University Press of America, 1982), 240, 241, 246–48.

41. *Rose Pastor Stokes* v. *United States*, Bill of Exceptions, In Error to the District Court of the United States, pp. 98–126, 135–53. A copy of the court transcript is included in the Rose Pastor Stokes Papers, Manuscripts and Archives, Yale University Library.

42. *Congressional Record*, Senate, May 31, 1918, pp. 7231, 7232.

43. See Woodrow Wilson to Atty. Gen. T. W. Gregory, June 24, 1918, Mail and Files Division, Department of Justice Records, File Number 9–19, National Archives. Wilson, while describing the conviction as "very just" also noted "the apparent injustice of convicting her when the editor of the *Kansas City Star* seems to be, to say the very least, a direct participant in her offense."

44. Alfred Bettman to Thomas W. Gregory, February 10, 1919, Gilbert Bettman Papers, Box 47, University of Cincinnati Library.

45. Rose Pastor Stokes to Mrs. Colt, July 6, 1918, Rose Pastor Stokes Papers, Tamiment Library, New York University.

46. *Stokes* v. *United States*, Brief for Plaintiff in Error. Copy located in Rose Pastor Stokes Papers, Manuscripts and Archives, Yale University Library, Box 9, Folder 13, p. 88.

47. *Stokes* v. *United States*, 264 F. 18 (1920) at 25, 26.

48. Philip S. Foner and Sally M. Miller, eds., *Kate Richards O'Hare: Selected Writings and Speeches* (Baton Rouge: Louisiana State University Press, 1982), 230.

49. See Sharp, "Rose Pastor Stokes," 141–54; David Karsner, *Debs: His Authorized Life and Letters* (New York: Boni and Liveright, 1919), 26.

50. Ray Ginger, *The Bending Cross: A Biography of Eugene V. Debs* (New Brunswick: Rutgers University Press, 1949), 346.

51. Eugene V. Debs to Rose Pastor Stokes, October 27, 1925, Rose Pastor Stokes Papers, Manuscripts and Archives, Yale University Library.

52. *New York Times*, February 17, June 15, 1919.

53. J. G. Phelps Stokes to Rose Pastor Stokes, 1925, Rose Pastor Stokes Papers, Manuscripts and Archives, Yale University Library.

54. Rose Pastor Stokes to J. G. Phelps Stokes, February 18, 1925, Rose Pastor Stokes Papers, Manuscripts and Archives, Yale University Library.

55. Rose Pastor Stokes, "There Are Few Bad Divorces," *Collier's* (February 13, 1926): 9, 49.

56. Quoted in Sharp, "Rose Pastor Stokes," 177.

57. See Rose Pastor Stokes, "The Communist International and the Negro," the *Worker*, March 10, 1923. Stokes was not a newcomer to the racial question, having participated in the 1909 Conference on the Condition of the Negro that led to the formation of the National Association for the Advancement of Colored People. See *New York Times*, June 1, 1909. In later years Stokes shared the Communist party's critical view of black reformists. Regarding W. E. B. Du Bois she was quoted as stating: "I found him a cold intellectual with frozen sympathies. He was perhaps the first black man to make me realize that not all men whose skins are black are oppressed proletarians; that the black like the white workers have in their midst the shrewd reformers concerned not with freeing the workers, but with keeping them in need of 'social service' which, like the Company Store, weaves about its victims an eternal web of debt and servitude." See Marguerite Young, "Rose Pastor Stokes," *New Masses* (June 1933): 23, 24.

58. Theodore Draper, *The Roots of American Communism* (New York: Viking, 1957), 387.

59. See "A Minority Report to be appended to Program and Methods of Approach," Rose Pastor Stokes Papers, Manuscripts and Archives, Yale University Library.

60. *New York Times*, April 15, 1933.

61. Rose Pastor Stokes to Maximillian Cohen, February 26, 1933, Rose Pastor Stokes Papers, Manuscripts and Archives, Yale University Library.

62. See *New York Times*, June 1, 1909.

63. See Patrick Renshaw, "Rose of the World: The Pastor-Stokes Marriage and the American Left, 1905–1925," *New York History* (October 1981): 415–438. The autobiography provided much of the basis for an interesting but somewhat speculative, psychoanalytically oriented, dissertation study of Rose Pastor

Stokes's life, up to the period of her affiliation with the Communist party. See Stanley Ray Tamarkin, "Rose Pastor Stokes: The Portrait of a Radical Woman, 1905–1919," Ph.D. dissertation Yale University, 1983.

64. Rose Pastor Stokes to Samuel Ornitz, December 15, 1932, Rose Pastor Stokes Papers, Manuscripts and Archives, Yale University Library.

65. See Samuel Ornitz, *Haunch Paunch and Jowl* (New York: Boni and Liveright, 1923).

66. Young, "Rose Pastor Stokes," 23.

67. Samuel Ornitz to Earl Browder, August 6, 1934, Rose Pastor Stokes Papers, Manuscripts and Archives, Yale University Library.

I. CHILDHOOD IN EUROPE

1. The reference is to a group of lakes in the Masuria region located in the northeast corner of contemporary Poland.

2. For a vivid portrayal of conditions in London's East End at the turn of the century see Jack London, *The People of the Abyss* (New York: Macmillan, 1903).

3. Between August 31 and November 9, 1888, an unidentified killer known as Jack the Ripper murdered five women living in the Whitechapel slum district of London.

II. COMING TO AMERICA

1. Castle Garden, located in Battery Park at the southernmost tip of Manhattan, served as the United States Government Immigrant Station from 1855 until in 1892 the agency was moved to Ellis Island. The immigrant novelist-journalist Abraham Cahan wrote of Castle Garden: "The stench was terrible as if a thousand cats were living there." See Ronald Sanders, *The Downtown Jews* (New York: Harper & Row, 1969), 41, 42.

2. Rose Pastor's employer was Isaac Brudno, born in the Belorussian city of Volozhin, who came to Cleveland in the 1880s or early 1890s. He established a cigar factory, the Imperial Leaf Tobacco Company, and later became involved in real estate development. A figure of note in the local Orthodox community, he died in 1914. See Dr. Eli Grad, comp., *The Brudno Family: A Family Tree and Biographical Sketches* (Boston, 1984), 62. Also see Joseph Morgenstern, "Cleveland Fifty Years Ago: Reminiscences of Immigrant Life," *Jewish Currents* (January 1958): 19–21, 46.

3. Ezra Selig Brudno was born in Volozhin on June 5, 1878, and after the Brudno family came to Cleveland he attended Yale University, Western Reserve University, and the Sorbonne. He began the practice of law in 1902 and served as assistant district attorney from 1910 to 1914. He also authored several novels and magazine articles about Jews and Judaism. Ezra Selig Brudno died in 1936. See Grad, *The Brudno Family*, 68.

4. David Edelstadt, born in 1866 in the Russian Pale, emigrated to the United States in 1882, first settling in Cincinnati and then moving to New York. He died of tuberculosis on October 17, 1892. Ronald Sanders writes of Edelstadt's poems: "The attempt they represent at reconstructing a folk diction on the basis of a radical political inspiration reflects the meeting of elements that constitute the beginning point of modern Yiddish poetry." Sanders, *The Downtown Jews*, 126.

5. Emile Vandervelde, *Collectivism and Industrial Evolution* (Chicago: Charles H. Kerr, 1901). For many years Professor of Political Economy at the University of Brussels, Vandervelde was a prominent leader of the socialist Second International, before and after World War I.

6. Markham's "The Man With the Hoe," inspired by Millet's painting, first appeared in the *San Francisco Examiner* in 1899. See Edwin Markham, *The Man With the Hoe and Other Poems* (New York: Doubleday, 1899). Also see Louis Filler, *The Unknown Edwin Markham: His Mystery and its Significance* (Yellow Springs, Ohio: Antioch Press, 1966).

7. Morris Rosenfeld, *Songs from the Ghetto* (Boston: Copland and Day, 1898; rpt. Gregg Press, 1970), includes "Songs of Labor." One of the poems in this collection, "In the Sweat-Shop," begins: "The machines in the shop roar so wildly that often I forget in the roar that I am. I am lost in the terrible tumult, my ego disappears, I am a machine. I work, and work, and work without end; I am busy, and busy at all times. For what? and for whom? I know not, I ask not! How should a machine ever come to think?" Regarding Rosenfeld see Hutchins Hapgood's classic, *The Spirit of the Ghetto* (New York: Funk and Wagnalls, 1909), 103–6. Also see Irving Howe, *World of Our Fathers* (New York: Harcourt Brace Jovanovich, 1976), 421–23.

8. Professor Hans Georg Dionysius Holfelder (1891–1944) was a prominent radiologist, known for having developed a technique for measuring radiation dosages. The assistance of Dr. Benjamin Felson, late Professor of Radiology

Emeritus, University of Cincinnati, in providing information about Professor Holfelder is gratefully acknowledged.

9. See *Jewish Daily News*, July 22, 1901.

III. JOURNALISM AND MARRIAGE

1. Something of what Rose Pastor Stokes might later view as a "traditional viewpoint" was expressed in a piece she wrote following the 1903 Kishineff pogrom in Russia. Kishineff, she wrote, "will be the bugle-call that will summon all American Jewry to enter the Zionist ranks to which it will respond with quickening pulse and leaping heart." See *Jewish Daily News*, June 9, 1903.

2. Naphtali Herz Imber (1856–1909) published "Hatikvah" in his first volume of poems (1884). Imber's last years were spent in poverty and alcoholism, relieved by some assistance from Judge Mayer Sulzberger. Even in this period, however, Imber eloquently expressed his social commitment. In his poem "My Muse" he wrote, "My muse is a true daughter of Israel, not a Greek Hetura, who sold her body to Plato and her soul to Jupiter. My muse gave her soul and body to the persecuted race, not flattering the rich, only consoling the poor and the oppressed with the words: 'Not is yet forlorn our hope.'" See *Jewish Daily News*, February 15, 1903.

3. Eliakum Zunser (1836–1913), born in Vilna in the Russian Pale, achieved repute as a wedding bard or "badkhn," improvising verses and melodies, combining the folk tradition with the skill of the artist. Emigrating to the United States in 1889 Zunser fused a nationalist spirit with the belief in socialism. For a portrayal of the later Zunser see Hapgood, *Spirit of the Ghetto*, 98–105. Also see Ronald Sanders, *Downtown Jews*, 130–34, and Sol Liptzin, *Eliakum Zunser: Poet of his People* (New York: Behrman House, 1950). There is a vivid portrayal of Zunser in the novelist Edward King's depiction of East Side life, *Joseph Zalmonah* (Ridgewood, N.J.: Gregg Press, 1968), 110–32, 217–19.

4. Nahum Meyer Shaikevich (1849–1905), writing under the pen name "Shomer," was the author of numerous novels and plays marked by the theme of the triumph of good over evil. His work encouraged the involvement of Jews in the affairs of the broader world. See Hapgood, *Spirit of the Ghetto*, 262–67.

5. See Rose Pastor, "The Views of a Settlement Worker: A Talk with J. G. Phelps Stokes," *Jewish Daily News*, clipping in Rose Pastor Stokes Papers, Box 6,

Manuscripts and Archives, Yale University Library. Stokes was reported as believing in the furtherance of movements "to better the condition of the working classes" and as wishing that none would suffer in consequence of the dislocations caused by progress. For a fictionalized version of Pastor's relationship with Stokes see Anzia Yezierska's *Salome of the Tenements* (New York: Boni and Liveright, 1923). Yezierska's biographer, Louise Levitas Henriksen, notes that it was "only the externals of Stokes's life and mannerisms . . . that went into the vivid personality Anzia created. . . ." See Louise Levitas Henriksen, *Anzia Yezierska: A Writer's Life* (New Brunswick: Rutgers University Press, 1988), 170–71.

6. Edward King (d. 1922) was a Scottish-born editor, writer, and labor activist who immersed himself in East Side life and became a popular lecturer at the Educational Alliance. Moses Rischin writes of King: "This tiny Scottish positivist, for a time the Central Labor Union's key figure, repeatedly brought East Side Labor's plight to the attention of the churches." See Moses Rischin, *The Promised City: New York's Jews, 1870–1914* (Cambridge, Mass.: Harvard University Press, 1962), 177. Ronald Sanders described King as someone "whose gentleness and simplicity of manner won him many admirers among the Jewish immigrants." Sanders, *Downtown Jews*, 67.

7. Margaret Wein, as Rose Pastor Stokes recalls her name, was actually Marguerite Vanvien, born in Paris in 1879, who had emigrated to the United States with her family. For a description of Vanvien see Marcelle Hertzog-Cachin, *Regards sur la vie de Marcel Cachin* (Paris: editions sociales, 1980), 53–61. Marguerite Vanvien's father took the name Wein upon emigrating to the United States in the late 1870s, so as to distinguish himself from his brothers. Docteur M. Hertzog-Cachin to Herbert Shapiro, August 25, 1988.

8. During 1904–1905, Ekaterina Constantinovna Breshko-Breshkovskaya visited the United States, addressing several large public meetings. For an account of this trip see Alice Stone Blackwell, ed., *The Little Grandmother of the Russian Revolution: Reminiscences and Letters of Catherine Breshkovsky* (Boston: Little, Brown, 1919), 111–32.

9. For a recollection of the Barrows family see Blackwell, *The Little Grandmother,* 125–29.

10. Stokes confused Edward Fitzgerald with the actual translator Sir Edwin Arnold.

11. Charles Sprague Smith (1853–1910), professor of modern languages and

literature at Columbia University, 1880–1891, served as managing director of the People's Institute at Cooper Union.

12. Sonya Levien (1898–1960), studied law at New York University and later became a successful Hollywood scriptwriter, with credits for such films as *State Fair, Oklahoma, Hunchback of Notre Dame, Lilliom,* and *Rebecca of Sunnybrook Farm.* She married Carl Hovey, a prominent New York magazine editor.

13. John Burns (1858–1943) had been a key leader of the 1889 London dock strike. Elected to Parliament in 1892, Burns served in Liberal administrations, holding the office of president of the Local Government Board from 1906 to 1914. Unwilling to support British entry into World War I, Burns resigned his cabinet post in 1914 and did not again hold public position. Even as early as 1889 Friedrich Engels wrote to Sorge: "I am not at all sure . . . that John Burns is not secretly prouder of his popularity with Cardinal Manning, the Lord Mayor and the bourgeoisie in general than of his popularity with his own class." See Kenneth D. Brown, *John Burns* (London: Royal Historical Society, 1977); also see E. P. Thompson, *William Morris* (New York: Pantheon, 1976), 328–30, 528–30 passim. In George Bernard Shaw's play *The Apple Cart,* Burns is the model for the character "Boanerges," the president of the board of trade in the cabinet of Prime Minister "Proteus."

14. Henry Codman Potter (1835–1909) was selected as Protestant Episcopal Church Bishop of New York in 1887. He was also the author of several books on religious topics.

15. Jacob Panken (1879–1968), first socialist judge in New York City, served for twenty years in the Domestic Relations Court. In this earlier radical career Panken participated in founding the Waistmakers Union from which came the International Ladies Garment Workers Union. In the mid 1950s Panken presided at hearings to determine custody of the sons of Ethel and Julius Rosenberg. Regarding this aspect of Panken's career see Robert and Michael Meeropol, *We Are Your Sons* (Boston: Houghton Mifflin, 1975), 247–55.

16. Charles William Eliot (1834–1926) served as president of Harvard University from 1869 until retirement in 1909. Known for having introduced the elective system at Harvard, Eliot was also influential in broadening the American secondary school curriculum. He was editor of the *Harvard Classics,* the "five-foot shelf of books" that for years set a standard for what the cultured individual was expected to have read. Regarding Eliot's trip to Tuskegee it is

noteworthy that following his return to Cambridge, Eliot wrote to Booker T. Washington criticizing the school's perpetuation of mediocrity and urging a modification of emphasis upon industrial training. Eliot wrote that he felt "some concern lest at Tuskegee their manual side had an excessive development as compared with the mental labor side, or, in other words, lest industrial training should unduly impair academic training." See Hugh Hawkins, *Between Harvard and America: The Educational Leadership of Charles W. Eliot* (New York: Oxford University Press, 1972); also see Charles W. Eliot to Booker T. Washington, September 7, 1906, and Charles W. Eliot to Booker T. Washington, September 7, 1906, Charles W. Eliot Papers, Harvard University Archives.

17. For an account of the 1892 Homestead steel strike, culminating in a July 6 pitched battle between strikers and Pinkerton men, see Philip S. Foner, *History of the Labor Movement in the United States* (New York: International Publishers, 1955), vol. 2, pp. 206–18.

18. The *Atlanta Constitution* reported the visit of the Carnegie party in considerable detail, noting the presence of Rose Pastor Stokes, described as the "famous New York Jewess." See *Atlanta Constitution*, April 7, 1906. Earlier, W. E. B. Du Bois was one of a number of Atlanta blacks who protested the policy of racial exclusion at the planned Carnegie Library. The petitioners declared: "If Atlanta wishes her colored children to grow up into law-abiding and self-respecting men and women she must do something to counteract the influences for evil which surround black boys and girls, by influences for good." It was further noted that if blacks were to be excluded "why call it a 'public' library at all, since the rich and not the poor, the strong and not the weak, whites and not blacks are to enjoy its benefits." See "Petition of Negroes to use the Carnegie Library" (1903?) in W. E. B. Du Bois Papers, University of Massachusetts Library, Series 1, Reel 1, microfilm edition.

IV. CAMPAIGNING FOR SOCIALISM

1. J. Stitt Wilson was elected mayor of Berkeley, California, in April 1911. He was a respected clergyman and eloquent orator whose election was facilitated by resentment at machine domination of Berkeley politics. See Ira B. Cross, "Socialism in California Municipalities," *National Municipal Review* 1 (October 1912): 611–19.

2. John Calvin Chase (b. 1870), a shoemaker by trade, had served as mayor of Haverhill, Massachusetts. He was reportedly the first socialist mayor of an American town. Following his 1906 gubernatorial campaign in New York, Chase served as assistant national secretary of the Socialist party.

3. Stokes's vision of socialism precluded any interest in reform. He told the interviewer that it was "far more important to stimulate the masses of the people to think these things out for themselves, than it is to secure some immediate alleviation of existing circumstances at the hands of so-called leaders." Stokes also observed, regarding Theodore Roosevelt, that if "he endeavors to make exploitation by the non-participating owning class less intolerable to the robbed workers, he will have to be regarded as an obstacle, rather than an aid to progress." See *New York Times*, October 23, 1910.

4. See Scott Nearing, *The Making of a Radical: A Political Autobiography* (New York: Harper & Row, 1972).

5. Inez Milholland Boissevain (1886–1916) was a lawyer, feminist, and suffragist who strongly identified with the rights of labor and came to embrace the cause of socialism. She was one of the peace advocates who participated in the 1915 peace ship voyage organized by Henry Ford. See Allen Churchill, *The Improper Bohemians* (New York: Dutton, 1959).

6. For brief biographical information concerning Williams and his recollection of the Bolshevik Revolution, see Albert Rhys Williams, *Journey into Revolution: Petrograd, 1917–1918* (Chicago: Quadrangle Books, 1969).

7. On January 26, 1906, an audience of some three thousand filled Yale University's Woolsey Hall to hear Jack London speak on the topic of "Revolution." London told the crowd that he saw in the university the counterpart of "the conservatism and unconcern of the American people toward those who are suffering, who are in want." He explained: "And so I became interested in an attempt to arouse in the minds of the young men of our universities an interest in the study of socialism. . . . We do not desire merely to make converts. . . . If collegians cannot fight for us, we want them to fight against us—of course, sincerely fight against us. But what we do not want is that which obtains today and has obtained in the past of the university, a mere deadness and unconcern and ignorance so far as socialism is concerned. Fight for us or fight against us! Raise your voices one way or the other; be alive!" London's message was: "The revolution is here, now. Stop it who can." For accounts of this London speech

see Philip S. Foner, ed., *Jack London/American Rebel* (New York: Citadel Press, 1964), 72–77; also Irving Stone, *Sailor on Horseback: The Biography of Jack London* (Boston: Houghton Mifflin, 1938), 220–22; and Joan London, *Jack London and His Times: An Unconventional Biography* (Seattle: University of Washington Press, 1968), pp. 301–3.

At a public meeting in New York's Grand Central Palace, J. G. Phelps Stokes declared that he did not agree with London that "the catastrophe which these things (the accumulation of wealth and power in the hands of the few, and the like) threaten will necessarily come upon us." Stokes, quoted in Joan London, *Jack London,* 302.

8. James Roscoe Day (1845–1923) was inaugurated as chancellor of Syracuse University in 1894 and served in that office until retiring in 1922. Ordained a Methodist clergyman in 1872, before coming to Syracuse, Day held a pastorate at New York's St. Paul Church, were he became a close friend of Standard Oil executive John D. Archbold.

9. John D. Archbold (1848–1916), who earlier fought Rockefeller's combination, the South Improvement Company, in 1911 became the president of the Standard Oil Company of New Jersey. A representative of Standard Oil at many public hearings, Archbold also served as president of the board of trustees of Syracuse University.

10. Rose Pastor Stokes spoke in Cincinnati on March 9, 1913, at the Jewish Settlement Auditorium. But the meeting to which she refers in her autobiography almost surely is that of March 20, 1915, held at Cincinnati's Sinton Hotel, under the auspices of the Hamilton County Suffrage Association. See Rose Pastor Stokes to J. G. Phelps Stokes, March 21, 1915, Rose Pastor Stokes Papers, Yale University Library; Rose Pastor Stokes note to J. G. Phelps Stokes, "Bulletin V," Rose Pastor Stokes Papers, Tamiment Library, New York University; also see *Cincinnati Enquirer,* March 21, 1915.

11. Byron Warren Valentine, ordained Baptist minister, served as president of Benedict College from 1911 to 1921. During her visit to Columbia, on one day Stokes spoke at the University of South Carolina chapel, at a black church, a chapel session at Benedict College, and finally at another meeting at the university. See Rose Pastor Stokes to J. G. Phelps Stokes, December 1, 1916, Rose Pastor Stokes Papers, Manuscripts and Archives, Yale University Library.

V. WAR

1. Jules Guesde (1845–1922) was a prominent leader of the French socialist movement, the Party Ouvrier Francais. He served as minister without portfolio in the war cabinets of 1914 and 1915.

2. The text quoted by Rose Pastor Stokes is that given by the *New York Sun*, December 20, 1915. A slightly different version of the speech is quoted in the *New York Times*, December 20, 1915. Also see Philip S. Foner, ed., *Helen Keller: Her Socialist Years* (New York: International Publishers, 1967), 73, 74; following the speech Rose Pastor Stokes wrote her friend Anna Strunsky Walling: "I wish you especially, Anna dear, could have heard Helen Keller last night. She is a miracle and we were all thrilled. . . ." Rose Pastor Stokes to Anna Strunsky Walling, December 29, 1915, Walling Papers, Huntington Library, San Marino.

3. See Barbara S. Kraft, *The Peace Ship: Henry Ford's Pacifist Adventure in the First World War* (New York: Macmillan, 1978).

4. Karl Liebknecht (1871–1919) and Rosa Luxemburg (1870?–1919) were founders in 1918 of the Spartacus group of revolutionaries from which emerged the Communist party of Germany. On January 15, 1919, Liebknecht and Luxemburg were seized and murdered by counterrevolutionary army officers.

5. J. G. Phelps Stokes was a leader among the pro-war ex-socialists whose activities extended to such ventures as the National party. As early as March 1917 Stokes had declared: "The present attitude of the Socialist Party against Universal Military Training and national defense is contrary to the traditional view of the party and the International Socialist Movement which have always favored strength as a deterrent to aggression by any would-be oppressor. . . . It is our duty to the cause of internationalism to support our government in defense of international law and order." The National party convened in Chicago on October 3–14, 1917, but by the spring of 1918 the organization, lacking any genuine labor support, began to deteriorate. See Kenneth E. Hendrickson, Jr., "The Pro-War Socialists, The Social Democratic League and the Ill-Fated Drive for Industrial Democracy in America, 1917–1920," *Labor History* (Summer 1970): 304–22. Hendrickson suggests that many of the pro-war socialists "had already come to doubt that socialism could survive in America unless its philosophy were greatly altered. . . . Party opposition to the war seemed to offer an excellent opportunity for the right wing to make use of patriotic fervor and rally socialists

and their sympathizers to the task of re-orientation. But it became clear that these defectors had nothing truly original to offer" (305).

    6. Robert Hunter (1874–1942) was a prominent socialist intellectual in the progressive era prior to World War I. See Hunter's classic study, *Poverty* (New York: Macmillan, 1904) and *Violence and the Labor Movement* (New York: Macmillan, 1914).

Index